Get Creative with Your Family History

Vicki Korn Niggemeyer

Cover design by Anne Gundersen

DENVER, COLORADO

Dedicated to my greatest supporters in life:
my Mother and Father, and my husband Chuck.

Contents

Why All the Fuss About Family History?

I have been interested in family history for many years. And since you have picked up this book, you obviously are also. Collecting family history is an exhilarating experience that typically starts with finding all those ancestors, then progressing to a method for putting the information into some kind of book or creative package for saving and sharing.

Many of us make such a fuss about family history because it is valuable to us. Knowing where we came from, and who we came from is interesting, exciting and could potentially prove to be valuable financially if you end up finding a long lost relative who is wealthy!

But don't count your cash just yet. The single, primary purpose for finding and recording family history is to preserve it for future generations. Along with that comes the satisfaction of discovering who we are related to, recording the events of their lives, saving their stories, placing our own lives into the long arc of history and recording it all for our children and grandchildren.

Many of you already have a working genealogy in progress, others may just be getting started. Either way, the principle purpose of this book is to provide all of you with some creative ideas for telling your family stories.

Here are four things you need to know, and think about, as you read this book.

1. For those of you who are new to the world of genealogy, the following paragraphs listing internet sites are the only references for tracing ancestry in this book. Subsequent chapters will provide tips for finding other family information along with details about packaging your family history in an interesting and creative manner.

Internet sources are prolific today, and have the added benefit of allowing us to trace our ancestors from the comfort of our homes. Some valuable sites are: Ancestry.com, Archives.com, rootsweb.ancestry.com, usgenweb.org, genealogy.com, worldvitalrecords.com, cyndislist.com and FamilySearch.org to name a few. You can also try putting a country name, or state within the United States, into any search engine followed by the words: digital genealogy records.

If you are looking for information about a specific ethnic origin, there are special sites available for you to investigate. Do a search on the internet by typing in any ethnicity followed by the words: genealogy sources. You will discover multiple sites pertinent to your search.

If you are African American you can go to www.afrigeneas.com/welcome.html. Another resource that would be helpful is the book *Black Roots: A Beginner's Guide To Tracing the African American Family Tree* by Tony Burroughs.

Two other sites that might be helpful for anyone working on a genealogy are: Find-A-Grave.com and familytreemagazine.com. Familytreemagazine.com offers tips and suggestions for finding resources. Some of these sites listed above are free, most charge a fee.

Finding the names and dates of our ancestors is the first vital step to putting together our history, but our family histories are far more than names and dates. I love adding stories and information that bring genealogical data to life. This book explores ways to find and include such information.

2. I am writing this book primarily for those who, like me, choose to record and present the family stories in a creative fashion and want to do the work themselves. It is fun and satisfying work.

I do give some examples in the book of internet services that will put together books, photo albums or other personally unique packages for you. But the goal here is to provide you with tools and suggestions to do the work yourself.

3. Computers are incredibly convenient, but not essential. Whether you are a savvy computer user, a beginner, or have no knowledge whatsoever, this book will give you ideas and directions for packaging your family history in a variety of creative forms.

References to computer software will be seen frequently throughout this book. I am not endorsing any specific software package. If you are already fluent with a specific software program, that is what you should use. If you do not already use a graphics based software package, you might want to consider shopping for a program that easily combines both text and graphics. I use examples within this book about the programs I am familiar with, but have also mentioned other software packages used by friends and family. If at all possible, you should use what you know and are comfortable with.

4. You should also think about how best to protect your work even before you start. Working on family genealogy is fun and satisfying, but it also takes time and effort. Before you begin working on your family keepsakes you may want to think about taking the proper steps to ensure the lasting preservation of your projects, photos and documents.

The internet has many reliable sources of information for protecting important documents and materials. Enter into a search engine the words: preserving historical documents. You will find many sites with instructions and merchandise available to assist in safeguarding your photos and family records. You will find that certain paper is better than others, certain glues are better to use than others, where to store your documents. A few other suggestions I found are: never use adhesive tape on photos, keep papers in a cool dry place, store documents flat if possible instead of folding, use plastic paper clips instead of metal, use acid free folders and boxes for storage. You will find plenty of advice to choose from as you work through the sites available.

Regardless of any other choice you make, do choose today to get your family story in writing! By making a fuss about your family history today, your descendants will thank you tomorrow.

Notes

Why Go Beyond Genealogy?

For those of us who value information about our heritage, genealogy is important. Genealogy tells us who we came from, our parents and grandparents. The lists of names and dates reveal numbers of siblings and children. Genealogy usually tells us where our ancestors came from. Sometimes occupations and other vital information are listed. But no matter how thorough, a genealogy is just the skeleton of any family story.

As you worked on your genealogy did you wonder what else there was to know about them? What were they really like? Were they straight-laced and serious? Or did they like to sing, maybe sit around the kitchen table and laugh? What did they like to do? What kinds of jobs did they have?

Maybe you don't have the answers to those questions. Then again, you may have more than you think. There are techniques that can help you enlarge the picture of who your ancestors were. The rest of this chapter addresses ways to add information to your genealogy and liven up your forefathers. And foremothers!

Add background information. Think of watching a play with no scenery or backdrop. Doesn't it feel like something is missing? Providing scenery to the family genealogy can have the same kind of effect. When I put together my husband's family history we were able to trace his ancestry back to 1780 in Paderborn, Germany, the name of his ancestor, his wife and one son. That was all we knew.

In my introduction to the family history, I included a map of Germany, pinpointing the city of Paderborn, and several paragraphs about the history of the city. I even found a photo of what the city looked like in the mid-1600s. By 1780, the feudal system of Medieval Europe was long gone and the Holy Roman Empire nearly at an end; the family had survived centuries of brutal living conditions. Adding background information provided concrete images of places where our ancestors lived and worked, giving some context to their lives which makes them seem more real to us.

Add a photo, or better yet, several photos if you have them of the people in the genealogy or places they lived. Photos bring tangible images that we can relate to. She had dark hair. Curly hair. He was tall.

Broad shouldered. He looks like he had a lot of physical strength. They lived on a farm. Wow, they had a Model-T!

Even photos have their limitations. This illustration is an old black and white photo which tells us very little about the gentleman. We can see that he is elderly. He had a beard and moustache. He was dressed nicely and appears to have been photographed in a studio, so he was obviously somewhat successful in life. He isn't smiling, yet I believe there is the tiniest trace of a grin behind that beard and moustache. By adding a story to go along with the photo we get a much clearer understanding of who this man was.

Young Samuel was only 18 when he left his home, his family and his friends. He enlisted in the Union Army serving in the 110th Regiment of the Ohio Volunteer Infantry, part of the Army of the Potomac under Generals Meade and Grant. We can only imagine how frightened he must have been as his regiment moved from Ohio into West Virginia and beyond.

It is not certain when, but we know for sure that at some point Samuel was captured by the Confederates. He spent a brief spell at Belle Isle Prison located near Richmond, Virginia. The island prison was built for 3,000 prisoners, but housed nearly 10,000. Conditions were brutal and deadly. Prisoners were allowed to swim in the James River and many tried to escape. Most didn't make it, but Samuel was one of the lucky ones.

He told his granddaughter years later: "I traveled during the night and hid during the day. I had a tin cup and used it to capture milk from cows along the way." Once he had left enemy territory the journey got a bit easier. "Sometimes a farmer's wife would see me and give me something to eat." Samuel finally made it safely back to Ohio. As he walked along Darby Road near Piqua, he saw the face of his beloved in the window of her home.

After rest and recuperation Samuel returned to his unit. He was

*wounded in the Battle of the Wilderness in May, 1864. Samuel recov-
ered and was honorably discharged in 1865. He and Hannah were
married in 1868.*

Where did this story come from? It is a combination of 13 percent
genealogy, 58 percent oral family history, 20 percent internet research
and 9 percent inference/conjecture from general historical knowledge
coupled with the first three categories.

The genealogy provided names, birthdates, the marriage date
and places the family resided. Family oral history provided Samuel's
Civil War experiences. Internet research provided specifics regarding the Ohio regiment's movement, when they left the city of Piqua
and details about Belle Isle Prison. With all the details at hand it is
easy to construe that Samuel was a frightened young man setting
off to war.

Other family research from the same time period leads me to believe that the family moved from Pennsylvania to Ohio in search of
more land, as did other branches of the family. When using inferences
it is important to make that clear in the story; I used the words *most
likely* when telling of their move from Pennsylvania to Ohio.

All of these elements: love, fear, challenge and a happy ending converge into a vibrant story that grabs one's interest. Not all stories have happy endings, but even the sad tales can be filled with informative, heart wrenching, realistic narratives of family members.

Maybe you are thinking, "But, I don't have any family stories that have been passed down over the years." Don't panic yet. You may have more information than you realize. When I wrote the story of my husband's family I had very little oral history prior to the 1900s. I did have a good genealogy and a few notes about where the family came from in Germany, plus the manifest entry from the ship that brought them to America. The rest was part conjecture and general historical knowledge. From those few pieces of information I put together six paragraphs about their journey from Germany to Ohio.

The population of Ohio grew steadily. By 1860, Ohio was the third largest state in America, trailing only New York and Pennsylvania. Of those two million inhabitants in Ohio, a whopping 83 percent were living on farms or in rural areas. Abraham Lincoln was elected president that same year, and the hearts and minds of Americans were heavy with fear as a Civil War seemed more and more likely. By 1860, a railroad system connected the major cities and areas of Ohio to the eastern part of the United States. Suddenly long distance travel was much easier and faster. More people were moving to Ohio.

On May 15, 1860, Jacob Niggemeyer and his family arrived in Baltimore, Maryland, on the ship Columbia. Like thousands of others coming to America, they were looking for a new place to call home. Jacob listed himself as a tailor, age 55, bound for Wheeling [WV]. The ship manifest lists the other family members as: Gertrude, 46, Jacob's wife; Johann, 16, (John B); Friedericke, 14; Theodor, 11; Heinrich, 7; and August, 5.

Daughters Carolina, 25, Theresa Gertrude, 23, and son Anthony N., 20, do not appear on that manifest, but they do appear in other family records suggesting that they came to America earlier than the others. From records we know that Jacob's oldest daughter, Carolina, went to Wheeling where she married Conrad Rolfe on November 1, 1857, three years before the rest of her family came to America. Theresa married Bernard J. Klingenberg on June 30, 1861, shortly after Jacob and his family arrived in America. There is no recorded explanation for how either of the young women might have met their husbands, but it is certainly within the realm of plausibility that one or both could have known their future husbands while still in Germany and traveled to America expressly to marry. Brother Anthony would have been a very appropriate chaperone and travel companion.

Did Carolina and Theresa's decision to come to America influence the rest of the family? Did neighbors in Germany talk about the opportunities in the new world stirring up ideas in Jacob's mind? Was Jacob tired of the tailoring business and ready to get back to his family roots, back to farming? Did Jacob long for land of his own? Land that he could not obtain in his homeland of Germany?

We will never know the reasons. Nothing was recorded and that part of the oral family history is long gone. So all we can do is speculate. Certainly all of the above possibilities are reasonable. We know that German immigrants were coming to America by the thousands. The opportunities of land and jobs in America were enticing. Once Carolina and Theresa made their decision to emigrate, it is not a giant leap to believe that Jacob and his wife would have been nudged to move the rest of the family also.

After arriving in America, Jacob, his wife, and their remaining five sons stayed in Wheeling for about seven years. Maybe Jacob worked as a tailor while in Wheeling. Maybe he was still searching for the right spot to buy land. Maybe he was in fact still yearning to get back to farming. Whatever the reasons, we do know that Jacob and five of his children moved to Athens County, Ohio, in 1867. After many miles and many years they had finally come "home" to Dog Hollow.

This particular story has no oral family history at all. It is composed of 19 percent general historical knowledge, 23 percent genealogy/manifest and 58 percent inference/conjecture. The genealogy provided the names, birthdates, death dates. The ship manifest provided the name of the ship, the dates of departure and arrival, and the names and professions of the passengers. Everything else was general knowledge of history, some internet searches and lots of putting the puzzle pieces together, or, in other words, inference and conjecture.

Are you thinking, "But, I can't write"? Okay, that's fair. Then again, you might be surprised at what you could put together. We're not striving for a Pulitzer Prize here; we are striving to put together an interesting, coherent family story that you can pass along to future generations.

"But, where do I start? What do I do?" In the following chapters we will explore many ways to tell your family story. You can put together a pictorial history using genealogy, photos, and bits and pieces of information. You can use timelines that list a chronological order of significant historical events and plug in your ancestors' birthdates, marriages and deaths thus constructing some historical context during their lifetimes. If you are really short on information you can put together a family historical calendar. What about making your own greeting cards that emphasize shared family history?

If you truly don't have old photos, stories from long ago, absolutely no information from past generations then start with today: yourself, your parents, your siblings. One hundred years from now your descendants will have lots of questions about you. Here's your chance to speak now and record your own stories and thoughts long before the questions arise. You may never hear the words, but certainly someone years from now will thank you for your efforts.

On the other hand, maybe you have lots and lots of photos. Maybe you even have some audio tapes or old family movies of your ancestors. Make a DVD complete with audio narrative. Liven it up with background music. Insert digitized documents. You can incorporate all kinds of material into a DVD then sit back and enjoy the show.

So why should we take the time and effort to go beyond the dull monotony of names and dates? Because the stories bring our ancestors to life! The stories put ancestors in a recognizable time period with specific events that they would have been aware of and lived through. The stories intensify their humanity. Even if you start with the current generation, your grandchildren, great-grandchildren and beyond will have a better understanding of who you were, the world you lived in and the kind of life you lived.

Getting creative with your family history should above all be fun, with the added benefit of creating tangible treasures. Whatever form you choose to use, your family stories will effectuate a connection to parents, grandparents, great-grandparents, cousins and relatives of long ago. Your efforts will also produce an enduring legacy for future generations.

You can do this! Let's get started.

Notes

Gathering Your Information

Assuming that you already have a completed or nearly completed genealogy you will want to start with that. Do you want to gather information about a specific person? A couple? Or do you want to gather information about the entire family? Pick a starting point and work from there.

As you gather information don't throw anything away! You may find information that at first glance seems irrelevant, but hang on to it. Somewhere on the notes make it clear who the notes pertain to, who you got the information from, a phone number or email address and the date. As your notes accumulate it can get confusing, so keep yourself sane and mark everything with names and dates. If you are working with multiple families, make a folder for each family and keep your notes in well-marked appropriate folders. Accordion folders are helpful if you have lots of photos and notes.

Now, here are eight suggestions to get you going.

1. Write down everything you already know.

Open a word document, or take out a pad of paper. Write down everything you know about your family: names, dates, places they lived, jobs they had, where they went to school, education levels, siblings, hobbies, interests. Anything at all that comes to your mind, write it down. Think back to when you were a child. Do you remember conversations about things your folks or grandparents remembered in their own childhood? Even if it's a brief sentence or a thought, write it down. Did they like to travel? Were they active in their community? If you remember a lot that's great. If you only remember bits and pieces don't get discouraged. It's a start.

2. Tap into the knowledge and memories of family and friends.

Have you asked other family members what they know about your shared ancestors? Are there other family members who are working on a genealogy? As that old saying goes, "two heads are better than one," so maybe you could collaborate.

Most of us have lots of relatives. Even if we don't have daily contact with them, we usually know where they live and how to reach them. In your search for family information, your family and friends will be valuable resources, so track down everyone you can think of.

I started working on my Dad's family history long before the age of email. I typed letters to my cousins and included information sheets. I asked a multitude of questions, like: What do you remember most about Grandma? About Grandpa? Do you have any specific memories of playing at the house, or in the barn? Describe both Grandma and Grandpa as you remember them. Do you remember any specific holidays at Grandma and Grandpa's home? And I always left a large blank space for individual ideas and memories. I also asked them to include any memories about uncles, aunts and cousins. I mailed the letters and included self-addressed, stamped envelopes for them to return the questionnaire. I really wanted them back!

I also asked for favorite photos. For anyone sending photos, have them put their name and address on the back of each photo and assure them you will return the photos. You can scan them yourself or have copies made. If you are doing your own scanning be sure that your scanner is set to the highest dpi for the best quality.

Today, communication channels are much quicker and easier thanks to email, instant messaging and texting on cell phones. The same questions can be asked. Photos or documents can be scanned and transmitted with a couple quick pushes of buttons. I put my husband's family history together several years after I did my Dad's family; being able to communicate via email made the process so much simpler.

Family members are the most likely sources, but they shouldn't be the only sources. Everyone has friends, co-workers, neighbors, people they knew at church or through other community organizations. Make a list and contact as many of these people as you can, or their children and grandchildren. Explain what you are doing. Most people are quite willing to share past experiences and talk about special friendships.

My Dad spent three years in the Army during WWII and the men developed long lasting relationships. They held annual reunions from 1947 up until the early 2000s. I was able to contact special buddies of his who provided me with information about their experiences during the war.

As you talk to family and friends they may be able to lead you to others who knew your parents, grandparents or whoever you are seeking information about.

3. Record conversations when possible.

Recorded conversations can be very useful and preserved for future generations of family history lovers. Of course the person you are talking to needs to be fully aware that you are recording him/her. Carefully identify each recording with the name of the person interviewed and the date. It may seem a bit stifling at first, but after a while the recorder often is forgotten and the conversation becomes relaxed and normal.

Recorded conversations can cover a wide range of topics and you will no doubt get more information than you think you want, but you might be surprised at how useful the interview can be in the long haul. Years ago I recorded a conversation with a distant cousin. I used bits and pieces of it soon thereafter, then put it away. Recently a friend was writing a book and quizzed me about some of our family history. I was able to pull that same tape out and extract some information that I had not been particularly interested in, but she needed.

You can use a magnetic tape recorder, but today's digital recorders are easier to use, render a better voice quality and can be directly downloaded to your computer. Whether you are using a magnetic recorder or a newer digital device, it is helpful to transcribe the contents into a written format, but it is definitely not necessary. Listen to the recordings and make notes if you don't want to transcribe the entire tape.

4. **Hunt for hidden treasures: diaries, journals, photos, family movies, letters, scrapbooks, photo albums.**

I realize that some families are savers, others are not. If you are not a saver, then hopefully someone in your family is and will allow you access to your family "treasures." If not, don't despair, you will still be able to put together something of value.

After the death of both of my parents, my brothers and I uncovered lots of "buried treasure." Not gold or jewels, but old diaries, journals, photos, letters, and calendars filled with events and appointments. At the time I was tempted to discard some of the things, but thankfully I did not.

Diaries are great. Even if the entries are sporadic with just a few words written, they are a window into what was happening in their day-to-day lives. The day WWII ended my Grandfather only worked part of the day. His August 14, 1945, diary entry simply reads: *"we worked two hours, at 6:50 o'clock the whistle blew for world peace, we went home. The war is over. It rained hard."* It was interesting and added a personal perspective to an epic historical event. I included that diary entry in the pictorial history of my mother's family.

Journals are also keys to unlocking our past. The trick is to wade through all the information that you may or may not need to get to the good stuff. And when you find the good stuff: highlight, highlight, highlight.

As I was putting together a pictorial history of my father, mother and my siblings, I was unable to put exact dates to the two homes we lived in. I remembered my father keeping all kinds of "useless" information in his journals: how much he paid for gas, groceries and other seemingly innocuous information. So I dug into his journals, and sure enough, I "struck gold." He had written down the dates when he purchased our very first home property (and the price), when he had poured the foundation of the home they built (and the cost), and the date we moved in.

Letters are almost as good as talking to someone. In the book I put together about my Dad's war experiences, I was able to quote from a letter his mother wrote to him when WWII ended: *"I am so glad and happy that the war is over...that your and Dick's lives have been spared.... I was just listening to the song,* Now the Lights Are on Again All Over the World. *It was very nice...."* It was almost as if I could hear her voice.

Calendars and day planners can also be useful in finding dates of key graduations, weddings, family reunions. It just takes time to wade through the information. Once again, highlight any items you think you will use.

Of course photos are the absolute best. Photos are the visible images of our families. They show us who they were; who we are. Formal photos are often of the entire family, taken on special occasions. Formal photos can also include images of weddings, confirmations, graduations. Informal snapshots get to the heart of the family by giving us glimpses of holidays, reunions, celebrations, sometimes even how they worked as well as how they played.

If old photos are not marked with names and dates it may be a bit frustrating to determine who is who. Host a family gathering. Maybe other family members can identify individuals in the pictures. Make notes on the backs of the photos with names, dates and the circumstances surrounding them if possible. Ask family members to bring photos, diaries, journals or other family related items that could add to your search. Ask about 16 or 8 millimeter family movies that were so popular in years gone by. Today's digital video camera footage can also be incorporated into a family history package.

Other sources for pictures that tell us about our family members are old school albums, church directories or other organizational scrapbooks. Class photos, ball team photos, home-ec or shop photos give clues about the interests of a family member. If you don't have albums of your own, check at the school or school library to see if they have any old ones tucked away. Church histories and directories should be accessible by asking the receptionist.

5. **Visit your local courthouse, historical society, local library and newspaper.**

Courthouse records are open to the public: property deeds, marriage licenses, birth and death certificates, plus many more. It may seem like these are more valuable in putting together the genealogy, and that is true, but the records can also assist in gleaning tidbits of our families' interests and achievements.

I spent two days in the Athens County Courthouse in Ohio searching through property deeds, marriage licenses, and birth and death certificates as I was preparing to put together a history of my husband's family. They had often talked about the one-room school my father-in-law attended as a boy. As I was combing through the deeds I found one that had recorded the sale of a half-acre of land from my father-in-law's grandfather to the Athens County Board of Education in June of 1881. Does that prove that his grandfather provided the land for the school? No, but the deed certainly establishes a reasonable likelihood that he could have. I stated so in the family history that there appeared to be a deep interest in education and that the land he sold *"is likely the site of Jasper Hill School where many of the Niggemeyer children were educated."*

Historical societies, some local libraries and local newspapers can also be of great help. Look for obituaries, wedding announcements, birth announcements. Check out the society columns as they too can sometimes provide clues about past activities and gatherings.

6. Use internet sources to help fill in the gaps.

I use the internet routinely to fill in the stories. After my Dad's death I decided to transcribe his war diaries. As I was working I began to wonder about the places he had trained, the places he was sent. I started doing some research on the internet. What started out as a very simple project turned into a 90-page book filled with his diary entries along with maps, photos, information about the bases where he trained and the three Pacific invasions he was a part of.

A tremendously wide variety of internet sources are available for anyone researching genealogy, military records, ship manifests and so much more. The internet can also be used to provide background information about places your ancestors have lived. Places they have worked. Interests and hobbies they may have engaged in.

Again, from my husband's family history, the only thing we knew about where his father worked during WWII was a snippet of information about the "TNT plant" in Point Pleasant, West Virginia. I plugged what little information I had into an internet search engine and came up with essential information about the West Virginia Ordinance

Works plant which turned into three paragraphs in the family history. Search engines are a marvelous tool.

7. Use timelines to provide context to your family story.

Timelines can be found on the internet. In the search box, type "timeline for 1944" and it will give you details and dates of historic events. Maybe you want to interject what was playing on the radio, so search under "music from 1944," it will give you a list of songs and who recorded them. You can do the same for movies, literature, sports or whatever category you and your family are interested in.

When I put together the *Korn Krops*, a history of my Dad's family, I used timelines at the end of each chapter and linked family events with specific historical events. My grandfather owned a lumber mill so I tailored that timeline to provide interesting events in the growth and development of the lumber business, interspersed with dates pertinent to the Korn Lumber Company. For the timeline following the chapter about my grandmother, I inserted historical events pertaining to women. (Examples of timelines can be found in Chapter 7.)

My early efforts at creating timelines took place before I had access to the internet. I love to search through bookstore bargain tables, and one day happened upon a book that I have used over and over through the years. It is called *The Timetables of History*, by Bernard

Grun, published by Simon & Schuster. If you are planning on doing lots of family historical writing, I would highly recommend finding a copy.

Family timelines are fun to put together. They provide a vivid glimpse of what our ancestors would have been talking about at the dinner table or over the fencepost with their neighbors. Timelines connect our ancestors to the bigger, broader picture of history. My grandmother was 42 years old when the Nineteenth Amendment was passed, allowing her to vote for the first time. My Uncle Fritz was born six weeks after the sinking of the Titanic. My Dad was seven years old when the Great Depression hit. My daughter was married on September 11, 1999, two years to the day before the attack on the World Trade Center. Their anniversary will always bring with it happy memories of the love that binds them together coupled with the shared sorrow of a tragic day remembered by the entire world.

None of us was born in a vacuum; the addition of timelines brings that into perspective. Local, state, national and world events are part of who we are and part of our stories.

8. Put the pieces together.

I talked in the first chapter about inference and conjecture. By definition both of these words pertain to the logical construction of a conclusion by drawing on incomplete or uncertain evidence. In other words: guesswork within the realm of logical possibility. If I put my fingers on the hot end of the curling iron, I will burn myself. But I don't actually have to do that to understand what will happen. If I drive my car to the grocery store and you see me coming out with bulging bags, you can pretty much determine that I have just bought groceries. You don't have to peer into the bags to know for sure. The same logical conclusions can be ascertained regarding our ancestors in certain circumstances.

Think about a period of time in history. The Civil War. We don't need to have first-hand knowledge to know that our ancestors lived through a terrible ordeal. Half or more of the country was a combat zone: the Virginias, Pennsylvania, Tennessee, the Carolinas, Georgia, to name a few. Everyone must have lived in constant fear of the dangers to themselves as well as their loved ones. They were probably terrified that they would lose their way of life, whether living in the south or the north. We can articulate those emotions because they are universal and timeless. So draw on your own emotions as you are telling the stories of your ancestors.

The huge wave of immigration is another chunk of history that includes many of us. From 1836 to 1914 more than 30 million Europeans migrated to the United States. (Check out the internet under "immigration waves.") The peak year was 1907 when a total of 1,285,349 persons came to America. If your ancestors arrived during that time span, you can automatically construe a couple of things: they probably came because of jobs and/or land; and/or, they came for better opportunities. You don't need an oral history in hand to know that.

If you are an African American with ancestors who were brought to America as slaves, you too can draw upon historical fact when envisioning and writing about the world your ancestors lived in.

Embellishment of a story can be risky. In telling our family story we need to be true to the facts, but there is nothing wrong with arriving at conclusions that align with what we already know about them and the world they lived in.

The above story of the Jasper Hill School is a case in point. As I searched through obituaries, news clippings, Lodi and Carthage township historical facts, I found the family name in a variety of places. They were extremely active in their church as well as civic affairs. So I believed I was on solid ground when I made the assumption that John B. fiercely supported a new school, to the point where he was willing to sell some land for it. The assumption was consistent with established facts about their role in their world. Even so, I always temper my conjectured conclusions with a resounding "this probably happened."

As you gather information about your family, explore every avenue possible. Talk to people, search the internet, read books about places they lived and the times when they lived. Even little bits and pieces of information develop into a vivid picture of your family when they are all put together.

I have often said at the end of a project that it was just like putting together a giant puzzle, and I love putting the pieces together!

Notes

Choosing the Method to Tell Your Story

Gathering your stories and material will never end. There's always more information out there. However, you will reach a point when you feel you are ready to move to the next step. That step is choosing the format for your story.

Before you can make that decision, you must consider four things: how much and what kinds of information you have gathered; assess the limitations of your skills, tools, time and interest; consider whether you will be making one copy for yourself, or multiple copies to share with your family; consider the cost in terms of time and money; then evaluate which specific format would be the best vehicle for telling your story.

Let's start with the information you have gathered. Have you organized your material so you truly know what and how much you have?

Genealogy and the resources that go along with it can take up lots of space. I know people who have closets full of three ring binders and shoe boxes full of information, photos and documents. But unless it is organized it can be tough to find specific items, and even tougher to figure out how much you might have for any given family or person.

If you already have your materials organized and catalogued, you are well on your way to having information at your fingertips. Maybe you already have well marked folders and three ring binders. Depending upon the numbers of folders and binders that you already have, a complete catalogue listing the folders/binders and location in your home can help save time and effort as you search for material.

After spending some time working on the *Korn Krops*, my first family endeavor, I decided pretty quickly that I needed to get myself organized. I gathered several boxes and placed them on the floor of the largest room in the house. During the sorting process I used shallow boxes that were a minimum of 8x10 in size, preferably a bit larger, like the bottoms and lids of large gift boxes. The larger size boxes hold large photos and documents. Next, I made index card tents by folding the cards in half. I wrote a family name on each card and placed it inside or close to the box for that family.

Then I brought all the individual boxes of photos into the living room. I sorted by family, placing the photos into the appropriately marked boxes. Depending on the number of photos you have it could be a lengthy process, but hang in there. It's worth it. Once you have all your photos distributed you can repeat the process with genealogy sheets, documents, notes, stories, whatever materials you have gathered. If your materials are mostly digitized versions, sort by family or individuals and place into marked folders.

The goal is to get everything you have about each family into one bundle; or, as in my case, drawers. I purchased plastic drawer sets, the inexpensive kind you can get at any discount store. I have a couple different sets: some have small drawers at the top and larger ones at the bottom; some have only the larger drawers. When I finished consolidating my material I made labels for the drawers so I could easily determine the contents. If you need more than one drawer for one family label it appropriately. Of course you could also use boxes, milk crates or any other kind of container to store your materials.

Refine the material as you place everything in the computer folders, drawers, boxes or crates. Use folders within folders for your computer material, manila envelopes or accordion folders for your physical photos and documents. I have envelopes in most of the drawers marked "documents." There were many pictures of my husband as a youngster, so I have two manila envelopes for him: one marked "early life," one marked "teen and college." As I was growing up we lived in two different houses, so I have a folder for each house. The more you refine and sort your materials the easier it will be to find exactly what you want when the time comes to use it.

Whether you choose to organize your materials electronically or tangibly, it is now time to take a critical look at what you have gathered. I suspect you will have more material for some family branches than others. At this point you should be able to assess more accurately the amount of information you have to work with and choose a format accordingly.

If you have an extraordinary amount of data you will probably want to choose a format that can encompass all of it, possibly a book length endeavor. If you have very little information you may want to do a simple scrapbook, a family calendar or greeting card. If you have plenty of photos and little information it is likely that a scrapbook or pictorial history would work best. If you have old family movies, video tapes and numerous photos you might want to consider making a DVD.

If you are doing multiple histories, one form may work better for one story while another format would be more suitable for a different story. I have completed six large family history projects: three have been book length narratives, two have been pictorial histories, and one was a mini book, more like a short non-fiction story. They have all been a bit different determined by the amount of information, oral history and photos at my disposal.

The amount of information you have gathered is just one aspect of this process. You also need to consider your skills, your time, your tools and your desire to complete this undertaking. How serious are you about wanting to create a tangible record of your family to be enjoyed today and saved for future generations? Are you willing to devote weeks, months, maybe even a year or longer to this project? Or would you prefer to put together something smaller that requires less time and effort?

Unless there is a compelling reason for haste you can take as much time as you need for your project. You don't have to do it in one week, or one month. My larger projects took a couple of years to complete as my work on the history was interspersed with family obligations. I feel comfortable putting the project away for weeks or a couple months at a time resuming work when it is convenient. I set what I consider to be realistic deadlines for my progress depending upon the external demands on my time. Write your deadlines on your calendar, or put them on the refrigerator as reminders to get back to your project. You do not want to put it away forever!

What about your skills? Do you like to write? Do you like to read? Do you enjoy surfing through information on the internet? Are you familiar and comfortable with researching other kinds of written materials?

Reading about the places and historical period in which your ancestors lived can be fascinating as well as productive. As you read, jot down information you might want to use. It is terribly frustrating to know you have written something down but cannot find it when you want it, so be sure to mark your notes with the source name, page number, a date, and place them with the appropriate family information. If you have gathered your information from an internet source, be sure to write the exact address on your notes.

Maybe you prefer working with pictures, or taking videos. My mother enjoyed putting together family photo albums with tidbits of historical information as well as names and dates. My husband does not write, but he definitely has a knack for putting together entertaining and engaging family movies. You want this to be an enjoyable project, so think carefully about your skills and interests so you can choose a format that will be fun for you to work on.

Your choice of a format will also be influenced by the tools you have. Do you have a computer? Good software? Scanner? Printer? Do you have beautiful handwriting? Know calligraphy? What about your work space? Is it convenient for spreading out your notes, photos and documents that you will need while you work?

Space is probably the easiest part of the equation to deal with. I am fortunate to have a large desk with a table nearby in our home office. A card table could temporarily be set up for the duration of your work. Dining room tables also provide large spaces for spreading out your notes, photos and documents.

Cutting and pasting formats obviously require very little in the way of tools. Creating family games, greeting cards, calendars, placemats, scrapbooks and pictorial histories are examples of family history pieces that can be put together inexpensively yet very creatively with scissors, glue, photos, typed or neatly written pieces of information and your own ingenuity. If you happen to already be a scrap-booker, or engage in stamp art, you will no doubt be able to come up with many clever ideas for your projects. If you want ideas for your pages, browse through scrapbook magazines or sites online that pertain to scrapbooking.

Larger formats are possible by using the cut and paste method. For many years handwritten or typed information were our only options, and they can still be used to create a cherished piece with personal handwritten touches. However, in today's world of high tech tools, a computer and good software make the projects much easier.

My first family book was done on Microsoft Word, a program designed to accommodate both text and graphics. If you are already familiar with Word and know how to construct pages with both text and graphics, then you will most likely want to use what you already know.

I switched to Publisher for my other projects as I found the program much easier to work with when combining graphics and text. PowerPoint, Print Shop and similar programs also offer good software packages for assembling pages with both text and graphics. Use what you are already comfortable with if possible.

If you have never used any of these software products, you might want to find a friend or family member who can help you get acquainted with some of these options. There are tutorials available when you buy software to help get you started.

Do you have a good scanner? Because I had both snapshots and slides, I bought a scanner that will digitize both. I can convert four slides at a time into digitized photos. Regular photos I scan one at a time. As I scan the photos I can sort them by family, vacation, location or whatever the criteria might be and put them into folders on the computer.

Do you have a good printer? If you do most of your creating on a computer you absolutely need a printer. We have a 3-in-1 printer which will print, copy and scan. If you have limited space, a 3-in-1 printer is a good solution.

In addition to skills and tools, you need to think about the number of copies you will need and the correlating costs involved. How many people in your family will want a copy? Will they be willing to reimburse you for the cost of putting it together? Will you want to copy everything in black and white to cut down on costs, or will you want to do some pictures in color? Will you want to print the manuscript on your own printer, or take it to a professional copying establishment? Check with your local print shops and get estimates. Your choice of format could be influenced by the cost involved.

When I had the *Korn Krops* published, I took the 109-page manuscript to a professional firm and had copies made with a spiral binding. Family members agreed beforehand to pay for their own books, which ended up being $15 per copy. I had it all done in black and white with no color photos as color increases the cost per book. At the same time we made a digital copy in the event I ran out of the hard copies.

I made far fewer copies of the Niggemeyer family history, and decided to print it at home on our own printer. I included many color photos and the quality was great. The ink cartridges were expensive; but I was extremely happy with the end result. My husband helped me collate and punch; then we inserted the pages into three-quarter inch, three-ring binders.

Even if you choose a cut and paste method for creating your family history, you will need to have copies of photos made if you are doing multiple books. Finding out the cost per photo beforehand could help determine the number of photos you will want to use.

Length of the manuscript also affects the cost. If you are having the manuscript printed for you, there is usually a price break after x-number of copies. If you are printing on your own, you need to think about the cost of ink cartridges. The more pages, the higher the cost. It is difficult to predetermine the exact length of any project, so don't be surprised it if ends up lengthier than you imagined.

Don't be afraid to ask your family members to share in the cost of the completed project. I was timid about that at first, but have discovered that most family members are quite willing to pay for their own copies. They are usually just happy that someone has taken the time to assemble a permanent record of the family history.

Keeping all of the above in mind, you are now ready to choose what kind of format will suit your material and your skills. Maybe you will decide to use multiple formats for different projects. Here are several options for you to consider. We'll go into the details of actually putting them together in subsequent chapters. For now, here is a list with brief descriptions of options I have used successfully.

1. Creating Family Games

Games can be very useful tools for teaching. Children and adults alike enjoy learning when it is fun. At your next reunion or family gathering offer a game that will playfully convey your family history. (Examples of games can be found in Chapter 5.)

2. Greeting Cards

Greeting cards can be made with the least amount of information and very little cost. Photos are perfect. You can use photos of individuals, homes, communities or images of anything reminiscent of your family. Add names, dates and a few tidbits of information to make your greeting card complete. It is a simple but interesting way to share family history with other members of your family. They also make great keepsakes.

Greeting cards can be sent for specific holidays or any time of the year. My grandmother, Gladys, was born on Valentine's Day, which makes for a perfect family history greeting card. But having a family member born on a holiday is not a prerequisite. You can send a family greeting card any day of the year. (An example of a greeting card can be found in Chapter 5.)

3. Placemats

Placemats can be given as gifts or used at your next family reunion. They are simple to make. Like the greeting cards, you can choose photos, historical information or copies of documents. You might choose to do a wedding placemat of your grandparents, including a copy of their wedding certificate. You might choose to do a placement of the old family home place. Placemats make great keepsakes and conversation starters at any family gathering. (Examples of placemats can be found in Chapter 5.)

4. Family Historical Calendar

Everyone uses calendars; they make great gifts and are an easy way to compile and display family history. I prefer making my own templates; however, you can find many pre-made templates within software programs or on the internet.

You can also choose services that will put your calendar together for you, for a fee, of course. Another option is to purchase inexpensive calendars at craft shops or office supply stores that have space for you to add your own pictures and information.

Calendars are the perfect fit for those of you who have limited photos and information. (Examples of calendars can be found in Chapter 5.)

5. Photo Album/Pictorial History

These two sound like they are the same thing, but I distinguish between the two by the amount of information each contains.

A photo album is primarily a book filled with pictures that have captions under each photo identifying the people, the place and the date the photo was taken. A pictorial history will have an abundance of photos but will include more text than a photo album. Pictorial histories could include copies of legal documents such as marriage, birth or death certificates; maps indicating where people lived; logos of places people worked; brochures and postcards of places they visited; and stories about their lives.

When I put together a pictorial history of my dad, mom and all three children, I included information about where my folks met and when they got married, information about his service in WWII, the church where all of us were baptized, confirmed and married. I used information from my dad's journals to track vacation dates and destinations, homes we had lived in. I also devoted pages for specific family celebrations such as my parents' 50th wedding anniversary party. I had multiple pictures for all of the pages as well as text describing different portions of our history. (Examples of photo albums and pictorial histories can be found in Chapter 6.)

6. Book Style

If you have a lot of information, multiple photos, documents, maps and other pertinent data, you may want to consider writing a book about your family. There are two types of books you can consider: a narrative or an unembellished compilation of information you have gathered.

Two of the family books I have written are narratives. That is, I wrote the material in a story-like manner. But you can also put together a book with little writing requirement of your own. Create your pages by using materials you already have on hand: photos, maps, copies of documents, newspaper articles, tidbits of local and historical events, quotations from letters and your own genealogy diagrams.

The book format requires a lot of time and devotion, but can bring a tremendous amount of satisfaction and joy when you see the finished product. It can be as long or as short as you want it to be. I've written four: three were between 90 and 130 pages long, the other was 20 pages.

If you don't have perfect grammar and spelling skills your family probably won't care. Having a detailed, written account of your family is what matters most.

7. DVD/movie/electronic scrapbook

Many of you may already be familiar with the versatility of PowerPoint. Not only does it have the capability to produce dynamic looking documents, it is also used by business professionals, teachers and other speakers who use visual pictures as teaching tools. Those same PowerPoint slides can be burned onto a DVD for viewing family history on any computer or TV screen. A variety of other software programs also produce electronic photo albums.

Making a DVD/movie/documentary is another electronic option. It is a time consuming venture, but the result will be a family classic that can be watched together in the comfort of your living room. If you are computer savvy, have a preponderance of photos, old movies, current digital footage, or audio tapes, you may want to consider putting together a DVD/movie about your family history. (Three examples of electronic albums/DVDs can be found by going to my website: getcreativewithyourfamilyhistory.com.)

As you consider all the format options above, be realistic about your skills, your time and the tools you have at hand to work with. You might want to start with a small project and work your way up to something larger.

Be realistic in your goals. You want to enjoy this adventure while realizing that the primary purpose is to create a lasting written and pictorial record of your family. It's important that you don't get discouraged and give up. So don't tackle a project that could become overwhelming to you. Keep it fun!

Allow yourself time to think through all of your options. Try to visualize the finished product. This is the beginning of a grand adventure. Plot your course wisely.

Fun Ways to Learn and Share

Playing Games

Many people consider history to be dull, boring, a waste of time. Even family history is a heavy dose of outdated data for some. But by livening up our history and making it fun, those of us who love our family stories can make it fun for others as well. Learning through games is a terrific way to impart and save family history.

My family has always loved playing games: cards, board games, charades. Our gatherings oftentimes get very loud with laughter. Even today a portion of our family gatherings is spent playing some kind of game for kids and adults alike. Here are a few examples.

"Who Am I?"

The object of this family game is to guess the name of an individual family member, a place or historical item from ten identifying pieces of information listed on a prepared game card.

In preparation, you will need to compile the data cards. You can hand write on an index card, or print from a computer. I made my game cards on a computer by dividing a letter size page into three columns. On each, place the name of a person, thing or place, and ten appropriate pieces of information for each card. Make several cards with a variety of family facts you want to share. An individual card might look something like this:

I am a person.

(answer is: William F. Korn)

1. *I lived in Montra, Ohio.*

2. *When I was a young boy I nearly cut off my foot when I landed on a scythe.*

3. *I used to play trombone in the community band.*

4. *I have a middle initial, but no middle name.*

5. *I am a man.*

6. *I owned a lumber company.*

7. *I finished eighth grade.*

8. *I died in 1956.*

9. *I loved going to the horse races at the county fairs.*

10. I am father to seven sons and one daughter.

Divide the family into two or more teams. Either the moderator, or a person from the opposing team, will draw a card with the family information. The moderator will announce only whether the card is about a person, a place, or a thing.

The team responding first will choose a number from one to ten. The moderator will read the answer and the guessing team will try to identify the person or object. If they do not guess at that time, they choose another number. They can continue to work through the numbers until all the clues from one to ten have been revealed. If the team still does not identify the name on the card, the other team gets one chance to guess.

The next card will go to a different team. You can assign a point system to the game and keep score, or just respond for fun.

Fun with Family Facts

Similar to the "Who Am I?" game, this requires preparation before the family gathering. Write out several questions with the answers on index cards, or print from your computer. The questions can be about individuals or families. For example: one question might seek four of the eight names of Bill and Neva's grandchildren. The team who is first could respond with all names. But if they can only come up with three names the question is then passed to the next team. A point system can be put in place to determine the winning team.

Kinfolk Quiz

This is an extremely easy game to offer at your next gathering. Have a prepared list of questions, photos or objects to identify, and let participants shout out the answers! Your questions will no doubt stir up other family facts as well, so be prepared for additional comments, stories and lots of laughter.

Be creative and make up your own games. There are many trivia types of games on the market that can inspire you.

Do not throw away any of the notes and cards when you are done. They are filled with valuable family facts, so you will want to save everything in a folder for future reference. You might even consider making games to give as gifts for those who could not attend; or use the same game again at future reunions.

Games can be fun and instructive at the same time. Games lead to dialogue about people, places, events that occurred in previous years. Games are a natural tool for teaching children. Adults, too, can learn from them while enjoying quality family time.

Greeting Cards

As much as I love my computer, emailing and the social networking available today, I am a throw back when it comes to sending greeting cards. I enjoy making my own cards, composing a hand written note and dropping the letter in an old fashioned mailbox. My family tells me they enjoy receiving them also. Adding family history is a bonus.

Once again, you have options. Pull out a commercial greeting card you have received and look it over. Typically a greeting card is folded book style with the opening on the right side of the card. Some cards are what I call tent style that are folded in the middle and open at the bottom of the card.

Choosing a card at a store provides you with many choices in sizes and styles. When I am making my own cards, I choose from one of two styles: either a four-fold opening on the right, or a tent style that can open at the bottom, when turned 90 degrees the tent style can also be opened on the right side of the card.

Now, take out a standard 8½ by 11 inch sheet of blank paper. If you hold the paper so that the 8½ inch width is at the top and bottom, that is called portrait orientation; if you turn it so that the 11 inch side is now at the top and bottom, the paper is then in landscape orientation. From the portrait orientation fold the card in half, top to bottom, then half again from side to side, so that it becomes a card size paper with four separate "pages." Write your name on each page and then unfold. You will notice that two of the pages will need to be printed upside down during the creating process, but once folded the pages are positioned correctly. It will look like this:

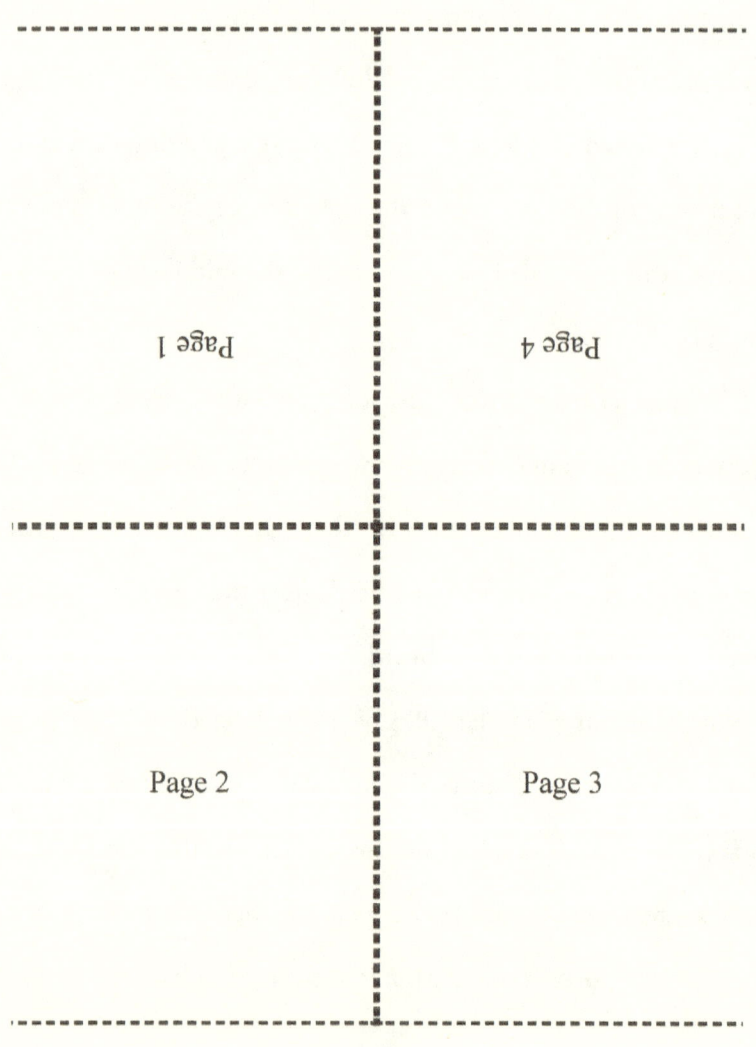

Repeat this process for a tent style card. Holding the 8½ x 11 inch paper in portrait orientation, fold it once from top to bottom. Again write your name on each page and notice that portions of the card will need to be created upside down. Now compare the two simulated cards. Do you need the larger format for the information you want to include, or will the smaller format be adequate?

Page 4

■■

Page 1

card printed on one sheet of paper.

Pages 2 and 3 are on the other side of the single sheet.

Do some doodling on the mock cards. Do you want to put a picture on it? If so, where? What do you want to say about your family member(s)? Remember to put your greeting line somewhere or write a little verse. Will your ideas work better on the smaller or the larger of the two formats? Work up a sketch of your ideas and see if you can determine what will make the most appealing design along with the historical details.

What kind of paper? A four-fold card works best using regular letter quality paper because it needs to be folded twice, but for the tent style I choose a card stock. I prefer white, but occasionally I will use a pastel color for certain holidays or occasions.

Folding letter quality paper is easy; getting the fold crisp and even on card stock can be trickier. I place the unfolded card stock on my paper cutter, lay a ruler at the half-way point of the paper and score along the fold line with an X-acto knife; use the backside of the blade and merely scratch the surface of the paper. Then fold. If the fold isn't precise I can trim the sides and bottom with the paper cutter. (If you are creating on the computer do not fold until after you have printed the card.)

Maybe you are thinking you can come up with your own size cards and unique formats. Terrific! Being creative with these projects is our quest. Do think also about envelopes for your cards. One of the reasons I use these two styles is the availability of envelopes for each size. Four-fold cards fit in standard invitation envelopes (4 3/8 by 5 3/4). For the tent style, I buy boxes of the greeting card envelopes (5 3/4 by 8 3/4).

Cut and Paste Method for Greeting Cards

Determine how many cards you want to make and the size. You can fold several of each size and have them ready. Choose the photo(s) you want to use and make as many copies as you need. If you are typing the historical facts make copies accordingly. If you are gifted with beautiful handwriting, or have learned calligraphy, you can hand write your greetings. I think you are ready. Assemble the materials you need and let your creativity flow!

Here are some things you will need:

- Regular 8½ x 11 inch letter quality paper
- Card stock in various colors
- Envelopes
- Scissors, glue, photo tape
- Photos
- Historical notes you want to share
- Fine tipped ink pen, calligraphy pens or markers in a variety of colors
- Things that might be helpful:

- Paper cutter

- X-acto knife (or similar tool)

- Art scissors to make design cuts

- Stickers

- Stamps and stamp art supplies

- Border art

Computer Design Method for Greeting Cards

If you are choosing to create your greeting cards on a computer, you still have some choices to make before you get started. There are many software packages on the market specifically for designing your own greeting cards that can be downloaded onto your computer. Or you can use the templates provided in nearly every general software package such as Publisher, MS Word, PowerPoint, Print Shop or similar programs.

If you choose to purchase a separate greeting card program, you can check online and read the reviews of a number of software packages; check out the specific functions that each program offers as well as the pricing. Just type in "greeting card software" in any search engine and you will see many sites including the review site. Before buying, you need to be sure the software is compatible with your home computer, and you will also want to make sure that the software program you purchase will allow you to import your own family photos.

If you already have software that includes a greeting card feature, you might want to start there. You will find greeting cards in a variety of sizes that are ready to print and mail. They can also be changed to fit your specific needs. You can delete what you want; keep what you want. Just click on the boxes provided and delete them, then add photos or text of your choice.

These same software programs provide templates for creating your cards from blank pages. When I open Publisher, I see a large variety of options available. By scrolling down that same page I eventually get to the greeting card section and find another large variety of sizes to choose from. Once you have chosen the card size you will be working on, the blank pages are already configured for a greeting card.

I have used three types of templates: those that are print ready with text and graphics, those that are configured but blank, or a template you create yourself. You can get some great ideas for your design from professionally prepared templates; on the other hand, you have the opportunity to create an expressly unique card if you start with a blank template.

To make your own computer template start by opening a new document in the portrait position. For a tent style card (folding top to bottom) you will need two pages to work with. The very first thing I do is to make the margins very narrow. Think about the fold of the card and understand that the top of the card will be the bottom once it is printed (remember the folding and doodling exercise). I start by making a large graphics box on the bottom half of the first page, then I add a decorative border. Inside that box I can add smaller boxes for photos or text. The top half of page one is the back of the card.

Handmade Just For You by Vickei

On the second page you will again need to envision the half-way point of the card from top to bottom. You can insert text or graphics boxes to give you a visual of the space you want to work with. Once your card is completed you will print on both sides of one sheet of cardstock.

Did you know:

Grandma Gladys was born on Valentines' Day, February 14, 1898.

Her father, William Franklin Pence, was also born on Valentine's Day, in 1869.

Grandma Gladys married Grandpa Carl Worthington on December 21, 1916.

After they married Grandpa always remembered her birthday with a large box of Valentine Candy. Both Neva and Evelyn remembered those beautifully decorated boxes of candy as far back as their memories would take them.

Grandma Gladys was very musical. She played the harpsichord, the piano, and even took violin lessons as a young girl. She loved to sing and the family gathered around the old piano many evenings: Neva said years later: "Mom would play the piano, I would sing the melody, Evelyn sang alto, Wig sang tenor and Daddy sang bass. Billy would just sing along."

During WWII Grandpa and Grandma had two of their children, a daughter-in-law, and all of their grandchildren living with them. They both had the gift of compassion, love and generosity in abundance.

Grandma Gladys died on July 9, 1983; and is still missed. We love you Grandma......

Valentine's Day is a reminder of all those we love and cherish,
Loved ones from today and yesterday.

Have a lovely Valentine's Day

Did you know that Grandma's favorite flowers were pansies?

If you are making a four-fold card you will need the same size blank page, 8½ x 11, in the portrait orientation. Mentally, or by using boxes, divide the page into four sections. Again, bring out the mock card and look at the unfolded page. Once the card is complete, but before you print, you will need to turn the contents of pages one and four upside down. Look on your toolbar to turn the boxes. This card will be printed on one side only of your paper.

For any of the above methods, using the mock cards we discussed earlier in the chapter is a great way to start solidifying your ideas. Make a rough sketch of the picture(s). Decide which position/location the picture will look the best. Where will you want the greeting? How much text do you want and where should it be placed?

I like to use attractive borders, especially on the fronts of the cards. The borders can be done in black or choose a bright color that will complement your graphics. Artsy graphics can also be interspersed with photos and history to dress up and give some color to your card. One of the best parts about using a computer is that you can easily delete and start over if you don't like the first attempt at a design.

Commercially prepared greeting cards always have a trademark on the back identifying the card company. I make my own by using a graphic image and printing below it, "handmade just for you by Vicki."

It's a simple and easy way to add a very distinctive touch to your hand-made cards. When using your own template you will need to turn the text and graphics on the last page upside down for it to be positioned correctly when printed.

Save your cards and templates. I have a folder on my computer just for my greeting card creations. I can use those same templates over and over again with a minimum of effort simply by changing text and graphics.

Once you have printed your cards you will need to score the card stock creations before folding. Lay the card flat, with a ruler at the half way point of the card, then score along the fold line with an X-acto knife; again, use the back side of the blade and merely scratch the surface of the paper. Fold. If the edges are not perfect, trim with a paper cutter.

Like any other endeavor, creating cards gets easier each time you make one. Now it's time to get started. Have fun!

Placemats

Placemats are probably the easiest to construct once you have chosen a family, person or place to focus on.

Fabric placemats typically measure 18 x 14 inches. When working with paper you can choose to create a custom size or use the 17 x 11 inch layout size which works quite well. After you have decided on the size of your layout, the next step is to choose the photos and materials you want to use.

Start by doodling on a scrap piece of paper to help visualize the completed project. I placed several photos at random leaving space for identifying text along with historical facts. Once you have an idea of placement you can begin cutting and pasting, or inserting photos to your computer page. I decided to place photos on both sides of the paper because I had so much information I wanted to include. Using one side only is certainly an option also.

When your placemat is completed you can print on your home printer, or take to a business store and have it copied and laminated.

Calendars

Before you start, remove a commercially prepared calendar from your wall and take a good look at it. It will have a cover page with a photo, the year, a business name and logo if it's for commercial advertising; sometimes a name or theme for the calendar is also evident. Inside the cover can be a couple pages with information for the business or it may just start immediately with the calendar pages. On the back of the calendar page is a photo or other information for the following month; the backside of the January calendar displays the photo design for February, etc.

If you have a booklet style calendar, look it over thoroughly also. Some will expand the calendar to cover both pages, but you have the option of using one side for the calendar and the facing side for photos and larger bodies of text.

The next step in the process is to make a rough draft of the events and pictures you will want to use. I make a rough draft for each month of the year listing important historical dates such as: births, deaths, weddings, major events in the community or church, the birth of a family business, family reunions - - any important event you want to include. Once I have the information gathered, I search for photos that will correspond with the events I am plugging into the calendar.

Decide what year you want to make your calendar. Typically I make my calendars as gifts, so I make them for the year coming up.

Spice up the pages with graphics. My maiden name is Korn, so for that branch of the family I used corn graphics throughout the calendar. Maybe your family loves animals, or has a favorite professional sports team, or a name like mine that is easy to absorb into the theme of the calendar. Many calendars use humorous or uplifting quotes. Does your family have some unique sayings that you could include? Use your imagination and have fun putting together a collection of historical facts, photos, individual family interests, recipes and humor.

Okay, I think you are now ready to choose which method will be the easiest for you to use: cut and paste or the computer.

Cut and Paste Method for Calendars

The cut and paste method for creating a family calendar is identical to the cut and paste method I described above for greeting cards. You can find suitable ready-made calendars in both craft and business stores. Some of these calendars are made specifically for adding your own photos, others have plenty of blank space to be filled in as you desire.

Assemble historical notes, photos, stickers, stamp art or other supplies you can use to embellish your pages. Either neatly print or type the information. Use both the facing page and the actual calendar to paste photos and bodies of text as space permits.

Computer Design Method for Calendars

For those of you who prefer creating your calendar on the computer, there is an array of calendar programs for you to choose from. Type in "make your own calendar" in any search engine. You can find several that will put your calendar together or offer designs that you can plug your specific material into. Some have the capability to add your own photos, others do not. Most of these sites charge a fee for the finished calendar.

Most software packages like MS Word, Publisher, PowerPoint, Print Shop or similar programs come with their own calendar templates; be sure to check them out. However, when I make calendars on the computer, I prefer to make my own template. It's easy, just a bit time consuming with your first effort. The best part is that I have complete control over the art work and the contents; plus, the templates can be used over and over again with adjustments made for dates, photos and information.

You can make your calendar booklet style or regular wall calendar style. Either design will be created using the same techniques. The difference will be the orientation of the pages. For a book style you will need to set the page orientation to the portrait setting. For the wall calendar use the landscape orientation.

The first page of your calendar will be the cover page. I like to use a card stock quality paper for the cover and the back page. I consider a nice large box with a decorative border to be perfect for the cover; smaller boxes can be placed inside the border for the calendar name, year, photos and a brief historical synopsis of the overall focus of the calendar. You can add some color to the font or the border. Add some graphics if you like. You want the cover to be attractive and interesting.

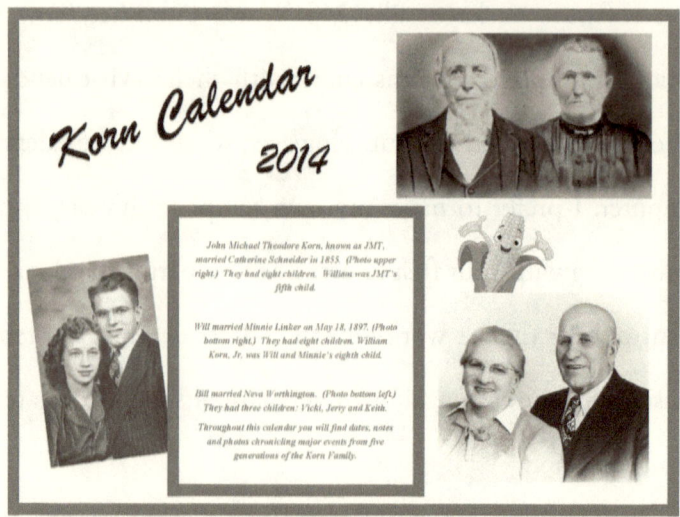

For the inside pages I use standard letter quality paper. I use the very first page inside the calendar as an introduction to the family. For the Korn calendar I included information about my great-grandfather who came to America in 1851. When you open the calendar this will be the first page you see.

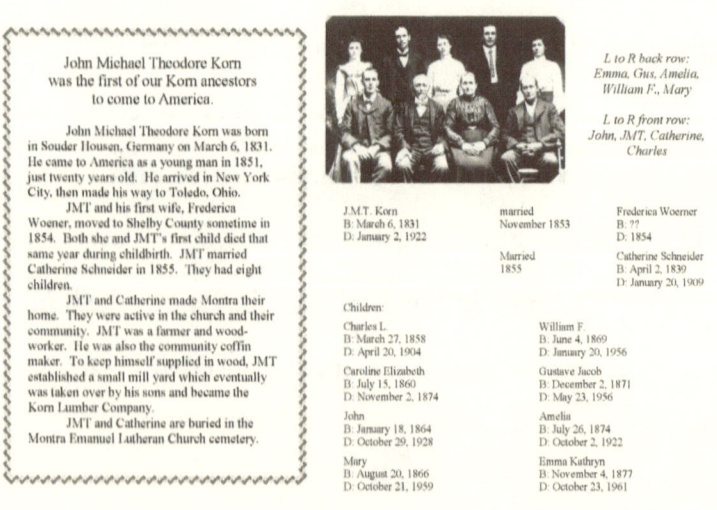

John Michael Theodore Korn was the first of our Korn ancestors to come to America.

John Michael Theodore Korn was born in Souder Housen, Germany on March 6, 1831. He came to America as a young man in 1851, just twenty years old. He arrived in New York City, then made his way to Toledo, Ohio.

JMT and his first wife, Frederica Woener, moved to Shelby County sometime in 1854. Both she and JMT's first child died that same year during childbirth. JMT married Catherine Schneider in 1855. They had eight children.

JMT and Catherine made Montra their home. They were active in the church and their community. JMT was a farmer and wood-worker. He was also the community coffin maker. To keep himself supplied in wood, JMT established a small mill yard which eventually was taken over by his sons and became the Korn Lumber Company.

JMT and Catherine are buried in the Montra Emanuel Lutheran Church cemetery.

L to R back row: Emma, Gus, Amelia, William F., Mary

L to R front row: John, JMT, Catherine, Charles

J.M.T. Korn
B: March 6, 1831
D: January 2, 1922

married November 1853

Married 1855

Frederica Woerner
B: ??
D: 1854

Catherine Schneider
B: April 2, 1839
D: January 20, 1909

Children:

Charles L.
B: March 27, 1858
D: April 20, 1904

Caroline Elizabeth
B: July 15, 1860
D: November 2, 1874

John
B: January 18, 1864
D: October 29, 1928

Mary
B: August 20, 1866
D: October 21, 1959

William F.
B: June 4, 1869
D: January 20, 1956

Gustave Jacob
B: December 2, 1871
D: May 23, 1956

Amelia
B: July 26, 1874
D: October 2, 1922

Emma Kathryn
B: November 4, 1877
D: October 23, 1961

FUN WAYS TO LEARN AND SHARE

The back of the first page will face the January calendar. Use this page for a collage of photos and text depicting the events covered in the January dates. You can include interesting borders and colorful graphics. Page three will be the first actual calendar page, January.

Montra, Ohio, the center of the world! At least it has seemed that way to dozens of Korn families since JMT and Catherine took up residence in the mid 1850s. Although many family members have spread their wings and moved to places all over the United States, there are still Korn family members who live in Montra today.

Reminiscent of old German communities, the tall spire of the only surviving church in Montra still stands tall, visible over all the other buildings. The church is a landmark and visible sign of the love and nurturing for all who have ever lived in this little Ohio country village.

JMT Korn was one of the founding members of that church. The group first met in an empty storeroom, then organized into a formal congregation on September 8, 1861. JMT was a primary builder and supplier of lumber for their first building. Twenty three members had collected $700 for the effort. In the winter of 1871 the church burned to the ground and once again JMT took charge. By fall of 1873 a new larger structure was opened on the site where the church stands today. For over 150 years Korn families have called the Montra Emanuel Lutheran Church their "home."

William F. Korn, 1955

Jerry William Korn, 1969

Sunday	Monday	Tuesday	Wednesday	Thursday	Friday	Saturday
January		1	2 1922, JMT died, age 91	3	4	5
6 1969, Jerry Korn joined the United States Air Force	7	8	9 1945: Bill Korn part of Luzon Invasion in Philippine Islands, WWII	10	11	12 1899: dedication of bell in the expanded and rebuilt belfry of Montra Church
13	14	15 1945: from Bill Korn's diary, "I got 56 letters today."	16	17	18	19
20 1909:Catherine died, age 70	21	22	23	24	25	26 1923: Neva Worthington Korn, born
27	28	29	30	31		

If you are using Publisher, MS Word or PowerPoint the following steps will be very similar with small differences depending on the software you are using.

To make your own template, start with a blank page on your computer screen. Adjust your margins where you want them to maximize your calendar space. If you are making the booklet style, you will want your left and right margins a bit larger to allow for collating and assembling the calendar pages. The same applies to the wall calendar except that the larger margins will need to be at the top and bottom of each page.

Looking at the blank page on your computer screen, which will be the third page in your calendar, go to the tool bar and insert a table. Choose a table format that will set off each box with a fine line border. Then select seven columns and six rows: seven days of the week, five weeks of the month, plus a row for labeling the days. The table will appear small.

By clicking and dragging, adjust the boxes to the appropriate sizes and expand to fill the entire space within your margins. The very top row of boxes should have just enough space to put in the days of the week. The rest of the boxes can be dragged out to larger sizes. Try to get the boxes equally sized. The clicking and dragging process can take several minutes until you get the exact sizes you want. Once your calendar page is sized, your template is ready to copy and paste onto subsequent pages.

Step one: insert a table with six rows and seven columns.

Step two: click and drag until the table stretches out to fit the page within your margins. Keep individual squares the same size except for the top row.

Sunday	Monday	Tuesday	Wednesday	Thursday	Friday	Saturday

Pull out a calendar with the dates for the year you want. In the back of my current calendar there is a small version for the following year. Plug in the dates for the month you are working on. Once the dates are placed in each box, you will notice that the first of January doesn't necessarily start on Sunday. In the following illustration, you can see that by masking out the lines separating Sunday and Monday, I have two blank spaces to use for the name of the month, or I can add quotes or graphics. Look at the end of January; it also has two spaces that do not have dates.

To mask out the unwanted lines, I insert two boxes. The first box is a regular text box, sized to fit the length and width of the two spaces I do not need for dates. In Publisher, even though I have a text box inserted into that space, the lines still show. So I click on the "fill color" button and click on "white," which masks the lines. Then I can add another text box within that same space and print the word January. The same process can be used at the end of the month for graphics or quotes. (If you are using MS Word or PowerPoint the lines behind the text box will not show, eliminating the need to fill in with white and add another text box.)

Step one: to mask the first two squares of this calendar, click on "insert text box."

Draw the box to fill in the two squares from top to bottom and side to side.

Notice, in Publisher the lines still show. If your program already blocks the line, then you can proceed to step three.

Sunday	Monday	Tuesday	Wednesday	Thursday	Friday	Saturday
		1	2	3	4	5
6	7	8	9	10	11	12

Step two: to eliminate the line in the middle of the two spaces, click on the text box and then click the "fill color" button and choose white.

Sunday	Monday	Tuesday	Wednesday	Thursday	Friday	Saturday
		1	2	3	4	5
6	7	8	9	10	11	12

Step three: click on "insert", click on "text box" one more time, then print the word January.

Sunday	Monday	Tuesday	Wednesday	Thursday	Friday	Saturday
January		1	2	3	4	5
6	7	8	9	10	11	12

Once your calendar is ready, type events and information you want to share into the individual boxes with dates. For example, on January 12, I typed in: "1899; dedication of bell in the expanded and rebuilt belfry of Montra Church." It's a tight space, so throw out the rules of grammar and just get as much info in as possible! For larger pieces of information that correlate to the month use the facing page.

At the very end of the calendar I inserted the family genealogy and some blank pages for recording future information. Family history is an ongoing project; give them room to keep adding.

Once your calendar is completely done, print your cover page separately; print the rest of the pages back to back. I like to laminate the front cover to make it sturdier. Arrange the pages in order and punch three holes in the proper margin: on the top for the landscape orientation, on the left for the booklet style. If you have made the wall style calendar, punch a single hole in the middle of each page for hanging. You can secure the pages with brads, small loose leaf binding rings, or you can give your creation a lovely look by threading a nice fine ribbon through the holes and tying it off with a bow. If you prefer, you can take your printed calendars to any office supply store and have them spiral bound.

Calendars are essential tools for our busy, busy lives. Now, with your one-of-a-kind calendar, it can also be a tool for preserving and passing along family history.

Making Photo Albums and Pictorial Histories

As I said earlier, there is very little difference between these two projects. Photo albums will have lots of pictures and limited text. Pictorial histories will have plenty of both: photos and text. Putting either one together requires the same skills and tools.

Photo albums can vary in size from a few pages of pictures to many pages of pictures. They can include other forms of memorabilia such as news clippings or copies of documents. Photo albums can contain various types of information with little text other than captions for the photos and memorabilia. The single quality that transforms an album to a pictorial history is the amount of text. In the largest pictorial history I have completed, there are 170 photos with many of those pages combining historical text along with appropriate pictures. That same pictorial history includes 26 pages of text alone: family stories, background, and genealogical information.

Living in the Anna House

Top left: The Anna House, Carl & Gladys working in the garden

Top right: Carl & Gladys Worthington

Bottom left: Judy and Vicki

Bottom right: Neva, Evelyn and Judy

Middle: Bill Worthington

The Earl Joshua Worthington Family

Earl Joshua Worthington and Myrtie Josephine Morris
Were married on January 1, 1895
They had six children:
Carl Morris, born on November 26, 1895
Johnie Silas, born on September 19, 1898
Bessie Hope born on November, 9, 1900
Horace Lowell, born on November 8, 1902
Vertie Frances, born on February 23, 1911
Lova Mae, born on April 21, 1914

Bessie Hope died shortly before her second birthday, September 26, 1902.

Front – Vertie, Grandpa Earl, Grandma Myrtie, Lova
Back – Horace, Carl, Johnie

The Earl Joshua Worthington Family lived in Miami County, Ohio, in "The Old Brick" where all five of the children were born. They moved to a larger house just up the road around 1915. Earl was a farmer and proud of his 6 foot height and physical brawn that came with it. Myrtie was qualified to teach grade school, but never did. She was happy to be a homemaker for her family, made wonderful angel food cakes, huge sugar cookies, and delightful pork roasts. Earl had high expectations for his family and all but Carl and Johnie went on to college. Earl was a tough man on the exterior, but a loving husband and father. He showed lots of affection to his family, especially his "little Myrtie." He was a Mason, he and his family were active in the Spring Creek Christian Church, and staunch Republicans.

Earl was born on January 20, 1875 and died on March 13, 1949; Myrtie Josephine Morris was born on March 6, 1876, and died on March 23, 1957. They are buried in the church cemetery in Fletcher, Ohio.

Earl's Father was Silas Anderson Worthington

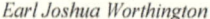

Earl Joshua Worthington   *Myrtie Josephine Morris Worthington*

Carl Morris Worthington: B: November 26, 1895; D: May 16, 1950
Johnie Silas Worthington: B: September 19, 1898; D: March 8, 1991
Bessie Hope Worthington: B: November 9, 1900; D: September 26, 1902
Horace Lowell Worthington: B: November 8, 1902; D: August 5, 1988
Vertie Frances Worthington Sands: B: February 23, 1911; D: July 27, 2004
Lova Mae Worthington: B: April 21, 1914; D: April 29, 2010

Here is an excerpt from one of the pages of text in that same pictorial history.

America entered WWII immediately after the surprise attack by Japan on Pearl Harbor, December 7, 1941. A year later, in December of 1942, Neva's husband, Bill Korn, was inducted into the army; Bill Worthington enlisted in the Navy in March of 1943; Wig entered the army on February 13, 1945. During that same period of time Evelyn and Alfred divorced. Off and on, for the next four years (1943 through 1946), there were several people living in one home. In 1945, while the men were off at war, there were nine people living together: Grandpa and Grandma; Lee, Butch and Billy Lee; Evelyn and Judy; Neva and Vicki. Judy remembers Grandpa and Grandma having the front of the first floor; Neva and Vicki lived in the back of the first floor; Evelyn and Judy, Lee and the boys living in the upstairs.

There had to have been days when such close living quarters, the stress of wondering about the men off at war, and the noise of four healthy, rambunctious young-ones became overwhelming. For the most part the memories are happy ones of congeniality and family harmony. But Grandpa's diary reveals that on August 19, 1945: "Mom had a nervous breakdown in evening." For the next five days, according to the diary, Grandma was "in bed." August 21: "Mom stayed in bed all day. Neva did our work." August 22: "Mom still in bed." August 23: "Mom still in bed." August 24, "Mom was up a bit and lay down two bits!" Grandpa's August 25 diary entry was back to normal stuff, Grandma was apparently up and okay!

Because the house was so large, and at that time nearly every room had a door, it was pretty easy to separate the living quarters. No doubt while Grandma was recuperating the doors were closed! That was the only recorded time frame during those years that Grandma or Grandpa buckled under the strain. Butch says he and his mother, Lee, both remember Grandpa as being quiet, agreeable, always in a cheerful mood and ready to help anybody. "Grandma was like a mother to Mom. She helped a lot taking care of us kids." Ditto for Judy.

By now you are getting an idea of the difference. And probably ready to think about your own projects. First of all define what your photo album or pictorial history will be about. One family? Multiple families? A specific family celebration? Do you want to do this in chronological order? Or would you like to feature individual family members one at a time? Maybe you will want to organize it by random family events.

Pull out the photos and information for your subject(s). The numbers and types of resources will steer you toward some ideas for your project. Envision what your book would look like. Write down your thoughts as a type of guideline. Now, do you want to make a photo album? Or do you want to put together a pictorial history?

If you have chosen to do a photo album, your next decision will be whether to have it done professionally or make it yourself. For example, Costco, Shutterfly, Blurb, Walgreens or Snapfish (just to name a few) all offer online sites for making your own personal photo book. Fees vary depending on size, number of pages, plus shipping and handling. Search the internet for a multitude of options; just type in "photo album books."

Once you choose a site you will have options for different covers, different layouts according to the numbers of pictures you want per page, different colored backgrounds. Some sites offer embellishments such as artistic graphics or quotes. My first endeavor was frustrating until I learned how to maneuver around the site. Eventually I figured out how to download the photos, choose from a number of layout options, and create the pages. Once I got the hang of it, it was pretty simple to use.

Professionally prepared photo books have the advantage of looking professionally done, obviously! They can be hard back or soft. They are colorful and pretty. You can find some sites that will print in sepia; if you are putting together a book of older family pictures the sepia will add to the historical expression of your album. Current events such as graduations, anniversaries, family celebrations of any kind can be recorded in one of these professionally prepared books and saved for future generations. After all, today's events are tomorrow's histories.

The biggest disadvantage, in my opinion, is that online books constrain one's creativity. I like to be able to assemble as many pictures as I want on each page. Often times the options available on the internet sites don't give me the freedom to construct the page as I envision. It works, but not always like I want it to. In other words, I like to have total control over the creativity of each page.

For either of these projects, photo album or pictorial history, choosing a suitable blank photo album could be challenging, but fun. You can shop online, or in a nearby store. Wherever you choose to shop, you will find a massive number of selections in nearly any color, theme, size or shape imaginable. It's wonderfully problematic. Do I choose this one? Or that one?

Photo albums range in types that include individual slots for 3x5, 4x6, 5x7 and even 8x10 photos. You can find albums that provide space for notes, others do not. If you are planning a standard family photo album any of these will work. Add identifying names, dates and events by typing or neatly printing the information and insert into the appropriate slot.

There are advantages in opting for a photo album of this sort. Most importantly, you can determine quite easily how many photos you will be able to use and how many slots will be left for text, portions of documents, newspaper clippings, or any other historical mementoes you may have. Count the slots. Count your photos. All remaining slots can then be used for inserting text and historical keepsakes. Neatly print names and events in the space provided, or type and insert into the photo slot along with the picture.

If you prefer to be a bit more creative with your album, you should choose an album that has full sized blank pages. Hard bound spiral albums cannot be expanded so are suitable for smaller projects. I prefer an 8x10 inch photo album that accommodates extra pages.

For the pictorial history of my Mother and Father, I chose a photo album that had pocket pages with an 8x10 sheet of white card stock in each pocket. I could pull the white card stock out of the pocket and create my pages, then re-insert into the clear, plastic pocket. You can add as many extra pages as you need within the album extension guidelines.

For my second pictorial history, because I had a lot of text as well as many photos, I decided to use a standard white three ring binder with a combination of two styles of pages inside. Most of the photos and small portions of text were placed on magnetic self-adhesive pages which have a clear overlay of plastic. One big advantage to using magnetic adhesive pages is that you can place different size photos along with bodies of text on one page and arrange them to your own style. Carefully pull back the plastic overlay to place your pictures and text, then carefully replace the overlay and press into place once the page has been constructed.

For my pages of text only, I used three-ring, clear plastic sheets of page protectors that you can find in any office supply store. You can insert typed pages, documents, old letters, news clippings, or other items and intersperse them with the other pages as they relate to your story.

The contents of both photo albums and pictorial histories can be arranged in a variety of ways. My first pictorial history was divided into sections. I had an introductory section with photos of my father, mother and the three of us children along with photos of the community where we lived. Then I inserted some photos and text about where my parents met and their courtship. Subsequent sections included my dad's war years, homes we lived in, the family business, the church we attended, Christmases and other celebrations, family vacations, grand-kids, and concluded with a section about the memory garden that Mother and Daddy planted and nurtured in their later years.

The sections I created were determined by the photos and documentation I had gathered. My collection of photos included many family vacation shots plus information from my dad's journals. There were lots of pictures of the homes we had lived in. It would have been interesting to include pictures and memories of the family pets we loved over the years, but I didn't have enough photos, so that was automatically eliminated.

You can tell your story in sections as I've described above, or choose to tell your story chronologically as I did with my second endeavor. Telling your story sequentially provides both flow and an automatic road map for you and the reader. Telling your story through special events has the advantage of highlighting the most important aspects of your family history.

Photo album? Pictorial history? One family? Several families? Chronological? Or family events? Think of it as standing in front of an ice cream counter - - which yummy flavor do I want? You get to choose.

Notes

You Too Can Write a Book!

Writing a book may sound intimidating to you. But don't be scared off yet. Even if you feel like you cannot write a book, you can put a book together using blocks of material, maps, genealogies and documents that will tell your family history for you. Your book can be short or lengthy depending on the amount of material you have as well as your vision for the story. Your book can be as creative or straightforward as you want it to be. You are the author, you get to choose.

First of all, determine the focus of your book. One family? Multiple families? Pull all the information from your files and do some preliminary studying. Think about how you see your book: chronological, in sections focusing on individual family members one at a time, thematically with an emphasis on careers or possibly by family events. Where do you want to start?

Secondly, organize your ideas. Most writers have learned a few tricks about organizing before starting the writing process. You are probably familiar with the journalists' litany of: who, what, where, when, why and how. All of those components can come into play when you are laying the groundwork for your family story.

When I wrote about my Dad's WWII experiences, my initial plan was merely to transcribe his war diaries. Very quickly I began to wonder <u>where</u> he had been sent. <u>Where</u> had he trained? <u>What</u> was his GI company like? <u>What</u> did they do? <u>Who</u> were the buddies he shared those memories with? <u>When</u> did he join? <u>When</u> was he discharged? Those questions can lead you to a workable outline of what you want to tell in your story.

Some writers use outlines. You no doubt remember from your school days that a formal outline defines key thoughts written down by using I, II, III, with subgroups defined within those categories by using A, B, C. Those subgroups can be extended even farther out by using 1, 2, 3. By using a formal outline you have a very detailed map of where you intend to go with your family story.

A rough outline is less definitive, but works well also. It would look more like an informal listing of thoughts. You might want to make a bubble outline with your central thought in the middle with spokes projecting outward defining specific thoughts and ideas. You can make several bubble outlines for each chapter or section of your story. I have often used a simple list of ideas that I want to cover, and then check them off as they are completed.

Plan, but be flexible. Whether you choose to use a detailed outline or a more relaxed style, understand that you can, and most likely will, deviate from your outline. I have never written any family history exactly as I first envisioned. As I work I find new information, find different sources with a different perspective, new maps, new documents. So I often find myself diverging to accommodate new thoughts and ideas.

Allow yourself time to merely think about your book. How do you see it in your mind? How do you envision your story progressing? I do a lot of writing in my head before I start putting it on paper. I often will have a pretty clear picture of where I want to go before I start.

Keep a pad of paper close by as you are going through the thinking process. Occasionally very precise titles, sentences or specific sequences of events will come to me and I know I need to write it down immediately. When I am in the middle of a writing project, I keep a pad of paper on my nightstand. Sometimes I will be thinking about my project as I am drifting off to sleep. Instead of jumping out of bed and going to my desk, I can record my thoughts on the notepad beside the bed.

Composing your story can be done by longhand on a pad of paper while sitting in an apple tree, like Jo of *Little Women*. But no doubt for our purposes the apple tree wouldn't be so comfortable, or conducive to good thought and effective work. You can record your family story by writing it in longhand, typing it on a conventional typewriter or make a voice recording and have someone else type it for you. On the other hand, I recommend working on a computer.

There are many benefits to working on a computer: a built in dictionary, a built in Thesaurus, spell check, grammar check and the ability to copy and paste text from page to page. I can easily move paragraphs from one spot to another. I can insert pictures, maps, documents or other materials easily into the pages of text. And by using a computer, once I have everything inserted and the writing refined, I am pretty much ready to print.

I have written one family book using Microsoft Word. The others I completed on Microsoft Publisher, mostly because I am so familiar with the program. Publisher easily accommodates both text and photos. My friend, Betty, used a combination of Word for the text and PowerPoint for the photos and documents when she did her nearly 400-page book.

If you have been using a specific software program, and feel completely at ease with it, that is what you should use. If you are not already familiar with a specific software package, I recommend choosing Publisher, Print Shop or any other software program that will easily accommodate both text and graphics.

Figuring out the mechanics is the easy part. The writing is the fun part. Once you have a clear outline of your story you can then think about the way you want to tell your story. If you prefer keeping your writing requirement to a minimum, you can merely enter information you have gathered, such as genealogies, documents, news articles, photos, maps, etc.

Another method is to write your story in a simple, straightforward narrative with little additional writing. Or you can embellish the story with interesting information relative to the time and place your family lived. This last method will require more writing on your part, but will result in a very interesting family history.

Here are three examples of these methods, starting with the minimal writing requirement by using materials you already have on hand.

John Michael Theodore (JMT) Korn	*married*	*Catherine Schneider*
B: March 6, 1831	*??/??/1855*	*B: April 2, 1839*
D: January 2, 1922		*D: January 20, 1909*

JMT and Catherine lived in Montra, Ohio. They had nine children:

Charles L.	*B: March 27, 1858*
	D: April 20, 1904
Caroline Elizabeth	*B: July 15, 1860*
	D: November 2, 1874
JohnB:	*January 18, 1864*
	D: October 29, 1928
MaryB:	*August 20, 1866*
	D: October 21, 1959
William F.	*B: June 4, 1869*
	D: January 20, 1956
Gustave Jacob	*B: December 2, 1871*
	D: May 23, 1956
Amelia	*B: July 26, 1874*
	D: October 2, 1922
Emma Kathryn	*B: November 4, 1877*
	D: October 23, 1961

JMT and Catherine's ninth child, according to oral family history, was a son named George. However, there are no records of his birth, death or grave site.

A simple, straightforward manner along with the above genealogy and a little embellishment might read like this:

My great-grandfather, John Michael Theodore Korn (JMT), was born in Souder Housen, Germany, on March 6, 1831. He came to America in 1851 and settled in Montra, Ohio. His first wife died in childbirth. He and his second wife had nine children, two of whom died in early childhood. JMT was a farmer, wood worker, and cabinet maker. He and his wife Catherine were pillars of the tiny Lutheran church they helped create in their little farming community in the Northwest corner of Ohio.

With a little more embellishment, you can impart that same set of facts interspersed with photos, genealogy, copies of documents along with other interesting elements to set the scene for your story. Embellishing the story might sound like this:

My great-grandfather, John Michael Theodore Korn (JMT), was born in Souder Housen, Germany, on March 6, 1831. In 1851, at the adventurous age of 20, JMT joined the second great wave of emigrants leaving his country and heading to America. From 1820 to 1870 they came to the United States, looking for new homes and opportunities. One third of those immigrants were German.

By 1852, train travel between New York and Chicago had expanded greatly opening up the mid-west to thousands of people looking for farm-land or new professions. Thus it was that by 1854, JMT had chosen to make Ohio his new home in a tiny little German farming community called Montra. JMT's first wife died in childbirth. He and his second wife, Catherine, had nine children, two of whom died in early childhood.

JMT was a farmer and wood worker. He was the village coffin mak-er as well as a cabinet maker. He was also one of the original builders of the tiny Lutheran Church that sat on the highest hill in the middle of the village. His constant demand for wood created a need for a sawmill which he founded then eventually turned over to three of his sons.

JMT lived to be 91 years old, spending the last 70 years of his life in the little village where he lived, worked and raised his family. He and his wife Catherine are buried in the Emanuel Lutheran Church cemetery in Montra.

As you can clearly see, all three of these methods get the message across to your readers. All three convey the information. You have to decide which method suits your style and your skills.

Whichever type of book you choose to write, a small book, a large book, a narrative or a straightforward factual book, you will most likely need to do some research. By far, the easiest to use is a search engine on your computer for finding pertinent information. Do an internet search using the name of your ancestor. You can plug in the names of cities, countries, organizations. You can find maps, photos, documents. In writing the above paragraph about my great-grandfather, JMT, I entered "immigration waves to America" and came up with information regarding the numbers of immigrants who came to the United States during that time frame.

I also turn to other sources as well, such as county court records, old newspapers, articles from genealogical groups, local historical societies. Your own folders are undoubtedly filled with some great items you can scan and include in your book, like news clippings, family photos, letters, post cards, family documents.

Another source is books. Yes, good old fashioned books! Because most of my family members settled in Ohio it certainly made my research a bit easier. I bought two books about Ohio history which I have used extensively. I also have a number of US history books that I use. When I do my research using books, I highlight and make notes in the margins. I often will use sticky notes to mark certain pages that have a lot of information.

My friend Betty put together two large books of family history: *The Life and Times of Walter White, 1880 – 1968* and *the Vaughan Wagon Train of 1847*. She is currently working on another book about her Uncle Ole Johansen, a sea captain. Betty found letters, journals, news clippings and other family mementoes that helped tell her stories. She also relied heavily on internet research.

Her books include a nice variety of photos, maps, letters, documents, news clippings, genealogical data and some words of her own to tell her stories. She did an outstanding job of putting it all together with little writing requirement, and produced a story that is interesting and easy to read. Below are four examples of her work.

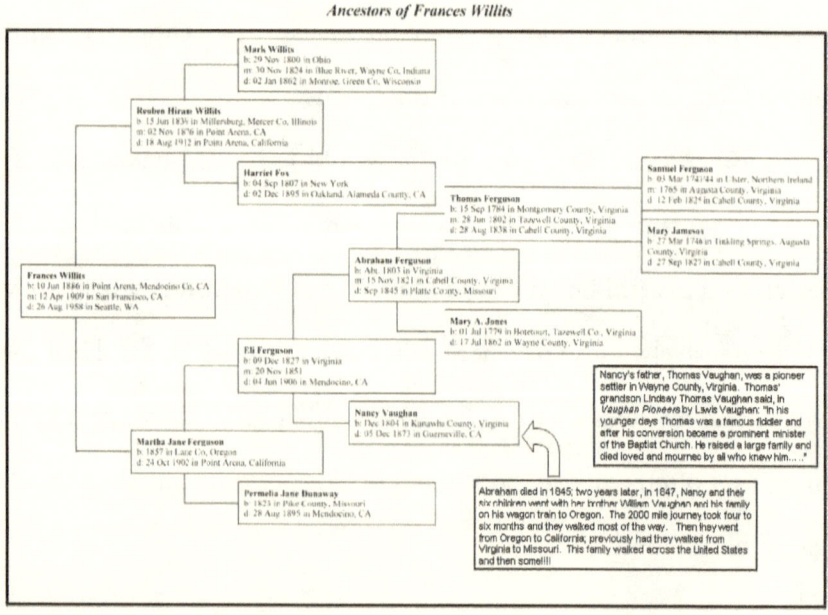

Ancestors of Frances Willits

March 1896 - Training Ship Warspite to 1897.
to 1903. Steamships and sailing Vessels.

Steamship Merrimac.	1897	O.S.	—	Foreign trade
Steamship Mary Anning.	1897	O.S.		Foreign "
Steamship Buckminster.	1898	O.S.		Foreign "
Sailing Vessel Nautilus	1899	A.B.		Coastal
Steamship Severn	1900	A.B.		Coastal
Sailing Vessel Hind	1901	A.B.		Coastal
Steamship Bardiston	1902	A.B.		Foreign "
Sailing Vessel Scottish Isles	1903	A.B.		Foreign "

(7 years)

August 1903. Steamship Minnewaska. 1903 Quartermaster Foreign "

Listed above are the ships Walter White trained or served on. O.S. is Ordinary Seaman; A.B. is Able Seaman, the next rank higher. His last position was as Quartermaster.

From Wikipedia: In the Royal Navy in the middle of the 18th century, the term **Ordinary Seaman** was used to refer to a seaman with between one and two years' experience at sea, who showed enough seamanship to be so rated by their captain. A seaman with less than a year's experience was referred to as a Landman, and one with more than two years' experience was referred to as an Able Seaman. Later, the term was formalized as a rating for the lowest normal grade of seaman. They are not trained in any special task. They are required to work at physically hard tasks of great variety. One needs an Ordinary Seaman Certificate to obtain work.

Able Seaman is a promotion from ordinary seaman.

Quartermaster: Aboard merchant ships, the term quartermaster usually refers to the experienced seamen assigned to bridge watches. The quartermaster's main task is to steer the ship and apply the helm orders given by the Captain or watchkeeping officers.

Capt. O. A. Joharsen lists the day and a short paragraph of activities and times. I am unsure of the ship and the purpose of his trips. I don't think he is fishing

In her book, *Seward, Alaska; A History of the Gateway City*, Mary J. Barry says, "He came to Resurrection Bay during the 1890s, bringing the first mining expeditions that landed there during the Kenai Peninsula gold rush." By 1896, the gold rush was on; a record amount of gold was found in 1897. He talks about "the mine," and "the cannery," he assists other ships, he carries passengers.

Ole Andreas Johansen
06 April 1866 – 30 March 1945

Ole Andreas Johansen was born on 06 April 1866 in Siljetro, Stjordal, Nord Trondelag, Norway. He died on 30 March 1945 in Seattle, Washington.

His father is Johan Arntsen Siljetro, born 29 October 1839 and died 1931; his occupation was a skipper.
His mother is Antonetta Taraldsdatter, born 23 September 1838 and died 27 September 1903. She is the daughter of Tarald Person As and Bergitte Andersdatter Velvangsoldra.

Johan Arntsen and Antonetta Taraldsdatter were married 13 September 1861 in Skatval, Nord Trondelag, Norway.

Ole married Mamie Smith on 10 June 1901. They had a daughter Henrietta.

Ole married Martine Sands on 1 January 1916.

There were ten children in this family:

Gjertrud Johansdtr, born 1861	Albert Gustav Johansen, born 1872
Berntine Johansdtr, born 1863	Johannes Johansen, born 1874
Ole Andreas Johansen, born 1866; died 1945	Anne Marta Johansdtr, born 1877
Peter Tobias Johansen, born 1867	Augusta Marie Johansen, born 1879
Johan Peter Johansen, born 1870	Peder Johansen, born 1882

Ships – I tried to match ships to years; this is the best I could do:
These four log books could all be from the Dora. *The Steamer Starr Arrives Here* says he was "Master of the **Dora** in 1897 for three years." He went from San Francisco to Sitka to Unalaska.
1897 – (April 6 to October 11, 1897 Log Book 1)
1898 – (April 6 to October 16, 1898 maybe Log Book 2)
1899 – **S. S. Dora** (March 17 to May 25, 1899 Log Book 3)
1899 - **S. S. Dora** - maybe(September 17 to October 30, 1899 Log Book 4)
(Captain of the Steamer **Bertha** for three years)
1901 – November 14; his divorce papers say he was "captain on the Steamship "**Bertha**" running between Seattle and the ports of Alaska"
1902 – Steamship **Bertha**, Capt Johansen, was wrecked in Fitzhugh Sound......
1903 – (June 1 to October 29, 1903 Log Book 5)
(1906 – Steamer Bertha was purchased from Alaska Commercial Co.)
1909, -10, -11 (January 5, 1909 to July 18, 1911 Log Book 6)
He was Master of the steamships **Chicago** and **Zapora** for five years each; in 1910 he was on the Chicago as he was in 1920 – per newspaper articles. Perhaps he switched back and forth.
1913 – 1914 – Fishing boat *Chicago* (February 25, 1913 to December 31, 1914 Log Book 7)
1921 – 1928 *S. S. Starr*

What can you legally use in your own manuscript when doing your research? I suspect everyone understands what plagiarism is. You cannot copy what others have written and pass it off as your own work. You can quote small pieces of someone else's work as long as you give that person credit. Gather the information and then rewrite it in your own words. You can use limited numbers of images from the internet as long as you notate where they came from and give that person or entity credit for their work.

How much material can you copy from the internet or other sources and place in your own work? The US Copyright Office has a site (www.copyright.gov/fls/fl102.html) that summarizes the Fair Use Doctrine. The Doctrine identifies four factors to be considered when deciding the legality of using internet or other public sources.

1. The purpose and character of the use, including whether such use is of commercial nature or is for nonprofit educational purposes
2. The nature of the copyrighted work
3. The amount and substantiality of the portion used in relation to the copyrighted work as a whole
4. The effect of the use upon the potential market for, or value of, the copyrighted work

Are you using the material for profit? Are you distributing the information to a small group of family members only? Are you giving credit to the authors or organizations who have put their work on the internet? Will your work infringe on the value of the original work? Go to the Copyright Site and read the Fair Use Doctrine. It should help you make the determination of how much material you can legally use.

In chapter two, I addressed the use of timelines as a technique for putting your family history into perspective. It is an easy way to bring ancestors to life through the window of specific events they would have lived through. If you have very few family stories, timelines are a way to add substance to your story. I use a combination of a timeline book called *Timetables of History*, by Bernard Grun, or I search the internet. Go to any search engine and type in the year(s) you are looking for. Some sites will list a variety of events for that year, some list music, sporting events, historic events.

In addition to straightforward timelines with family dates and historic events, you can also interject themes into your family timelines. In *Korn Krops,* I used dates from the lumber business in my grandfather's timeline, the chapter about my grandmother focused on events impacting women. It is not necessary to mix historic events with your family timeline, you can merely list the highlights of your family's history by the dates of their events. Here are five illustrations of time-lines you can draw from, the first four from my own manuscripts, the last one done by my friend Betty.

JMT Korn Family Timeline

1831	John Michael Theodore Korn, born in Souder Housen, Germany, March 6
1839	Catherine Schneider Korn born in Clay Township. Auglaize County, April 2
1851	JMT came to America
1853	JMT came to Shelby County, Ohio
1855	JMT and Catherine were married
1858	Charles Korn born, April 20
1860	Caroline Korn born, July 15
1864	John Korn born, January 18
1866	Mary Korn born, August 20
1869	William F. Korn born, June 4
1871	Gus Korn born, December 2
1874	Amelia Korn born, July 26
1874	Caroline died on November 2, at 14 years of age
1877	Emma Korn born, November 4

Korn/Ohio Timeline

1747	The Ohio Company was organized to colonize the Ohio River Valley
1788	First permanent white settlement in Ohio established in Marietta
1803	Ohio became the 17th state, March 1
1822	Ulysses S. Grant born on April 27, 18th US President, first to be born in Ohio
1831	**John Michael Theodore Korn, born in Souder Housen, Germany, March 6**
1832	Ohio and Erie Canal completed
1839	**Catherine Schneider Korn born in Clay Township. Auglaize County, April 2**
1849	Village of Montra first surveyed
1851	**JMT came to America**
1854	First recorded frame house built in Montra
1855	**JMT and Catherine were married**
1858	**Charles Korn born, April 20**
1860	**Caroline Korn born, July 15**
1861	Civil War began, April 12
1864	**John Korn born, January 18**
1865	Civil War ended, April 9
1866	**Mary Korn born, August 20**
1869	**William F. Korn born, June 4**
1869	Cincinnati Red Stockings became first all-professional baseball team
1871	**Gus Korn born, December 2**
1874	**Amelia Korn born, July 26**
1877	**Emma Korn born, November 4**

History of Lumber Business and Korn Lumber Company

1328   Invention of the sawmill

1620   Early American settlers establishing mills

1698   Invention of the steam engine

1808   Invention of the band saw, England

1814   Circular headsaw introduced in America

1857   Frederick Weyerhaeuser bought his first sawmill. Went on to become the biggest holder of forests and lumber mills in the United States.

1882   Forestry Congress, later knows as the American Forestry Assoc., first met in Cincinnati

1885   Division of Forestry instituted by US government

1894   Korn Lumber Company officially founded by John, Charles and Wm.

1897   US Forest Reserves first authorized

1904   William became sole owner of Korn Lumber Company

1939   First addition to Korn Lumber Company, building of a ware house

1947   Korn Lumber company converted from steam power to electricity

1990   August 25, Korn Lumber Company sold at auction after 96 years of business

Improvements for Grandma Minnie and Many Others

1793	Invention of the cotton gin by Eli Whitney
1810	Canning method discovered by Nicolas Appert, France
1820	Canning industry first brought to America
1820	Susan B. Anthony born
1825	First patent for the "tin can"
1834	First "crude" sewing machine
1841	First university degrees granted to women in America
1851	First continuous stitch sewing machine, I.M. Singer
1878	**Wilhelmina (Minnie) Kathryn Linker born, November 2**
1884	Eleanor Roosevelt born, October 11
1890	First Home Economics Classes taught in public schools
1909	**Catherine Schneider Korn (Minnie's mother-in-law) died, January 20**
1921	First US election in which women were able to vote
1939	Nylon stockings first appear on market
1974	Little League Baseball, Inc., votes to allow girls to play on its teams
1981	Sandra Day O'Connor becomes first woman Supreme Court Judge

1900

- Eli Ferguson is living in Arena Township.

The 1900 census shows Eli Ferguson, 72, living in Arena Township, Mendocino County, California. He is widowed, a farmer; he owns his own home, a farm, free of mortgage. There are no children listed as living with him.

- Martha Willits is living in San Francisco with her five children.

The 1900 census shows Martha Willits, 41, living at 938 Harrison, San Francisco, California. She is listed as head of house. Living with her is Lena, 19, a shipping clerk; Georgie, 16, a shipping clerk; Frances, 13; Fred 11; and Elva, 5. Martha is renting a house. The census says Martha had 7 children, 5 are living (William Mark was born in 1879; he would have been 21 in 1900 and he is not listed here.) Where is Reuben?

1902
The Great Register
Reuben Hiram Willits is in the 1902 Great Register; he is 64; his local residence is Point Arena.

October 24, 1902 – Martha Ferguson Willits passes away in Point Arena.

1906
Eli Ferguson dies:
Ukiah Republican Press - June 15, 1906, Ukiah, California
"Death of a Coaster.
"On Monday, June 4, Eli Ferguson died at the home of his daughter, Mrs. Robert Dickie at Point Arena, says the Record. Deceased had been under the care of a physician for the last month and succumbed to heart failure. Eli Ferguson was born in Wain county, West Virginia, on December 9, 1827. He came to California forty-one years ago and followed the occupation of farmer. He was the father of a large family and lost his wife some years ago. The funeral took place Wednesday from the residence of Mr. and Mrs. Robert Dickie, Rev. J W. Edgar conducting the services. The remains were laid away in Evergreen cemetery in the presence of a large number of friends and acquaintances."

1910
The Great Register.
Reuben Hiram Willits, Rollerville, 71, Laborer, Post Office is Point Arena.
Fred Willits, Rollerville, 21, Laborer, Post Office is Point Arena.

- Abraham D. Ferguson (Martha J. Ferguson Willits' brother) and his family are living in Arena Township, CA

The 1910 census shows Abraham D. Ferguson, 50, head of the house, living on Lighthouse Road, Arena Township, Mendocino County, California. He is a teamster, working at a lumber mill. He lives with his wife, Annie, 40, and their six children: William R. 22 – woodsman, tie maker; Lola L., 16; Mildred H., 15; Mary A, 10; Doris E., 7; and an adopted daughter Dorothy, 2. All children (except unknown for Dorothy) were born in California. The census says they have had 7 children and 7 are living. They are renting their home.

- Reuben H. Willits living in Arena Township, CA

Living a few doors down is Reuben H. Willits, 70, head of house and widowed; he is a farm laborer. Living with him are Fred, 21, single and a farm laborer; and Elva, 15. He rents his home.

Now, I think the following is really neat!

Living next down to Reuben (and Elva) is Porter O'Neal, 64, head of the house and divorced; he is a farmer. The census says he was born in Indiana; his parents were born in Indiana. He owns his farm. Living with him are his sons, Thomas, 27, a farm laborer (born in California) and Walter P., 16 (born in California). Why is this neat? Elva marries Tom O'Neal but not until many years later as we find her in the 1920 census living with her brother Fred; she is single.

- Lena and Edward Malinoff are married and living in San Francisco.

The 1910 census shows Lena Willits, 29, married to Edward Malinoff, 28. He is head of the house, and proprieter of a fruit store. They have been married seven years and have two children, Olga, 5, and Melvin, 4. They are renting their home – 1147 Golden Gate Avenue, San Francisco.

- Georgie Hazel and David Cohn are married and live in San Francisco

The 1910 census shows David Cohn, 33 and head of the house, and Hazel, 25, are living at 1121 Golden Gate Avenue, San Francisco (just a few doors down from Ed and Lena). They have been married eight years. David came to the United States in 1878 from Germany and has been naturalized. He is a bartender at a saloon; they rent their home. David and Georgie drown in 1916.

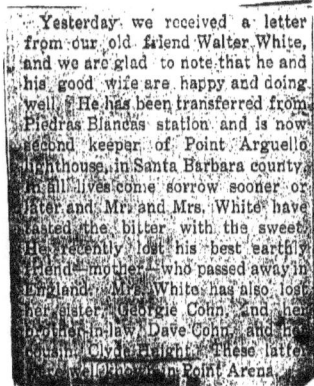

Yesterday we received a letter from our old friend Walter White, and we are glad to note that he and his good wife are happy and doing well. He has been transferred from Piedras Blancas station and is now second keeper of Point Arguello lighthouse, in Santa Barbara county. In all lives come sorrow sooner or later and Mr. and Mrs. White have tasted the bitter with the sweet. He recently lost his best earthly friend—mother—who passed away in England. Mrs. White has also lost her sister, Georgie Cohn, and her brother-in-law, Dave Cohn, and her son Clyde White. These latter belonged in Point Arena.

UKIAH REPUBLICAN PRESS
24 OCT 1902

POINT ARENA RECORD.
Mrs. Rube Willits was brought in from San Francisco last week. The lady is very sick and the children came up Tuesday to see their mother.
Mr. and Mrs. Smith who have been visiting in and around Point Arena the past four weeks, returned to their home in San Francisco on Wednesday's boat.

Martha passed away on Friday, October 24, 1902 In Pt. Arena, CA Clipping found at Ukiah Historical Society.

There was no date on this newspaper clipping which was glued in Grandpa's album but we know that:

1. He worked at Point Arguello from January 22, 1916 – July 20, 1920

1. Emily Packham White passed away on February 17, 1916

1912

Reuben Hiram Willits dies on August 18, 1912. He was 73 years old.

Saved by Walter White is the following article from a Pt Arena Newspaper:

Sudden Death.

Another of Point Arena's pioneers, old veteran and a good citizen has passed away. On Sunday morning the friends of R. H. Willits, familiarly known to all, as "Rube," were shocked to hear that he had been found dead in bed by his daughter Elva, having been stricken by an attack of apoplexy during the night, and tranquilly, as in a sleep, passed beyond.

Rueben Hiram Willits was born June 15, 1839, in Mercer county, Illinois, where he spent his earlier days, and at the time of his death was 73 years, 2 months and 3 days old. At the outbreak of the Civil War, Mr. Willits enlisted with the 140th Regiment, Illinois Infantry, and served his country faithfully from 1861 to 1864, when he was mustered out. He saw active service and was with General "Pap" Thomas at the battle of Lookout Mountain, one of the famous and hardest fought battles of the war. Deceased was among the last of the surviving member of G. A. R. Post of this place, now thinned by removals and death, there being seven left, five of whom acted as pallbearers at the funeral.

Mr. Willits was a resident of Point Arena for 39 years, coming here in 1873, and for twelve years conducted a barber shop in the building now occupied by E. F. Williford. He was married Sept. 2, 1876, to Miss Martha Ferguson, who died some years ago. By this union, there were five children who survive him —one son and four daughters, Mrs. Ed Malinoff, Mrs. David Cohn, of San Francisco, and Mrs. Walter White, Miss Elva and Fred Willits of Point Arena.

The funeral occurred Tuesday afternoon from the family residence on Mill street, Rev. D. Munro conducting the services, and was attended by a large circle of friends and acquaintances, who paid their last tribute of respect to a pioneer, old soldier and a good citizen. The interment was made in the Odd Fellows cemetery.

We wish to thank our friends and neighbors who extended their sympathy and kind assistance at the time of our sad bereavement.

Walter White and Family.
Fred and Elva Willits.

Incorporate family interests into your work. When I wrote the history of my husband's family I included recipes, some going back 100 years. When I put together the *Korn Krops* I included art work that my mother sketched specifically for the book, including a large image of corn fields and a farm house that I used for the cover. Family traditions, recipes, art work and unique expressions can help convey the character of your family; by interspersing them into your manuscript it will preserve them for future generations.

As you write, don't get hung up about grammar and punctuation. If you have questions you can find sites on the internet that will help you. Look for punctuation guidelines or rules of grammar. There are many sites available to help you. However, always keep in mind that the main purpose of your effort is to get your family history recorded. Your family will be happy just to have something in writing.

Are you numbering your pages? If the book is lengthy, numbering the pages is essential. Look at any professionally bound book in your home. Notice that page one is always on the right hand side; so odd numbered pages will be on the right, even numbered pages on the left. If you include pages prior to the first page of text you do not need to number those pages; for example, an introductory page or your table of contents do not typically have numbers, or might have lower case Roman numerals.

I always begin my family history with a title page followed by a short introduction. I thank all who provided stories, pictures, genealogy, or helped in any way. Your name and the date you finished the manuscript should be placed under the title, or below the introductory paragraphs. Give everyone credit, especially yourself!

Is a Table of Contents necessary? How long is your book? If your book is short you probably don't need one. However, if your book is lengthy and separated into chapters then a table of contents would be helpful to your readers.

If you are writing a book with lots of researched information you might want to include a bibliography at the end of the book. Why? Providing a bibliography does two things. It first of all authenticates that your historical information is based on fact, not just your thoughts. Secondly, a bibliography identifies your sources in the event that family and subsequent generations might want to refer to them for extended research. I do not use footnotes in my family books, but I have included bibliographies. Don't worry if your bibliography is not in perfect form, but do list the book titles and internet sources that you used along with authors and internet addresses.

After all your hard work, you will want to think carefully about the printing process for your labor of love. Once again, your decision will be influenced by how many copies you want and the costs involved.

Professionally bound books will nearly always give you the best results, but will also cost the most. Locally owned print shops are also a good option, but you will need to be careful in choosing which one will give you the best quality for the price. Doing the printing on your own computer is also a consideration. Compare all your options carefully. Professionally bound books are quite appealing. They have colorful covers, neatly bound pages, and look like a "real" book. To investigate companies and their costs type into any search engine "self-publishing companies." A myriad of choices will be presented to you. Lulu, Blurb and Outskirts Press are just three examples of companies that offer self-publishing. Pricing will vary by company, the length of your book and the number of books you need.

When I published Korn Krops, I used a locally owned print shop, as did my friend Betty. We both chose spiral bindings and used heavy cardstock for the covers. We both were required to convert our manuscripts into PDFs (Portable Document Format) to have them printed exactly as we designed the pages.

Before you contract to have the entire book printed have the shop print one or two pages to make sure the quality is acceptable; make sure at least one page contains a photo or two. Don't be afraid to go to another print shop if you don't like the quality offered at the first place. Be sure to get a price quote for the numbers of books you need and compare with other shops. Get an estimate of the time it will take to have your book ready for pick up.

If you elect to do the printing yourself, you can still have a quality heirloom. I have not had a family member yet who objected to the way I chose to print our stories! I have printed two lengthy books on a home printer. For the slightly smaller book, I bought covers at a business store that had brads already inserted into the binding. I printed the pages on two sides then used a three-hole punch and inserted the pages into the cover. For the larger book, I bought three-quarter inch, three-ring binders and inserted the pages.

If you opt to do your own printing, you will need to think about the cost. My first book had a few pictures in color, many pictures in black and white, and contained more text than graphics; so the total cost was reasonable. The second book I printed contained many color photos and was much more expensive in terms of the ink cartridges I needed. How many books do you need? How many pages are in your book? That too influences the bottom line cost. If your family shares in the printing cost that is quite helpful, so do not be shy about asking them to pay the cost for their own copies.

Regardless of your printing option choice, before you begin printing you will need to prepare your manuscript. If you choose to use two different types of software to build one manuscript, one for text and one for graphics, you will need to merge the two and then convert everything into a PDF when it is time to print.

Commercial printers will most likely require the manuscript be converted into a PDF to ensure the pages print exactly as you put them together. You can download your manuscript to a disc or a thumb drive and take it to the print shop.

If you are printing at home, you can print straight from your completed pages without a conversion process. I keep each manuscript in a separate folder, and I use one type of software per manuscript which greatly simplifies the printing process.

Writing a book about your family history will take some time, but will reap great rewards. The most difficult part is the very first page. Looking at that blank page can be daunting. But please don't let that stop you. Write down any thoughts that come to you. Write a paragraph. Write a page. Record those rambling thoughts as fast as they come to you. Oftentimes I write such gibberish that I nearly laugh out loud when I read it. Or groan! Then again, oftentimes within that gibberish there is a nugget of something that is usable. And that's a substantial starting point.

Notes

Your Family Story on the Big Screen

Up to this point, the focus of this book has been on traditional methods of preserving family history through print medium. This chapter will deal with newer concepts of putting our stories, photos and documentation into digitized formats for viewing. It is possible to display your family photos in video photo albums. It is possible to produce your own family story as a documentary/movie and save it on a DVD for easy viewing. Anything you use in a traditional photo album can also be placed into a digital project to be watched on a TV screen or your computer.

As the keepers of our family histories we are blessed to live in such a technologically advanced era. We have the ability to capture images, voices, resurrect family movies from years gone by and place them all in digitized formats. We can add music to the background. We can narrate our stories while at the same time showing documents, maps and photos corresponding to that narration. We have the ability to make family movies that could rival an Oscar winning documentary. Well, maybe not quite that good; but certainly good enough to be of interest and cherished by our families.

Like any other project we have explored in this book, the first thing you will need to do for any digital project is to have your information organized and ready to go. Identify the photos, documents, or images you want to include. Make sure all of these items are scanned and digitized before you begin.

Place everything relating to each specific project in one folder on your computer. Within that folder create sub-folders. For example, when I put together the Worthington pictorial history I had one folder on my desktop called Worthington history. Within that folder are sub-folders that contain text, scans, photos, first drafts and work sheets. One folder. Easily accessible.

Some of you have old family films you will probably want to include in your electronic photo projects. These films need to be converted to a digital format prior to starting any project. If you are interested in learning how to convert your movies yourself, enter into your search engine: "digitizing 16mm/8mm film." Directions for doing the work yourself are available online, along with an array of affordable conversion products. However, the process is time consuming and does not always render quality images. This may be one place you will want to spend the money for a first-rate transition from old film to a newer digitized format.

There are many professional film conversion companies listed on the internet: OldMovieConversion.com, MyMovieTransfer.com, got-memories.com, and iMemories.com are just a few of the companies to choose from. Pricing is variable. Some have minimum orders. Check out these and other online sites to find the company you feel will do the best job for you.

Some of you have audio recordings you will want to include in your project. I have several tapes that I made when my mother-in-law was still living. It is not only fun, but very satisfying historically to actually hear the voices of loved ones as we look at their pictures. Saving their voices is just one more aspect of preserving our history.

If you have a voice recorder that will transfer audio directly to your computer, that is wonderful. Download the conversations and interviews saving them in well-marked folders. If you are unable to download your audio tapes directly, there are internet sites with helpful hints or services to digitize your tapes for a fee, search under: "tape to CD/DVD."

Once you have all of your images, documents, video and audio excerpts organized, you are ready to think about what kind of digital project you want to create.

PowerPoint is a commonly used program and easy to learn. Many professionals use PowerPoint for slide presentations; it can also produce a digital family photo album. Other types of software can be purchased such as Flip Album and Smilebox for simple family photo projects. Search under "making photo albums on DVD" and you will find lots of programs to choose from.

Another commonly used video tool is Windows Movie Maker. This program allows for more creativity than PowerPoint. You can insert video clips along with your photos and images of documents. You can also add music and narration.

For an even more elaborate documentary style video you might want to explore video software options from companies like Pinnacle, Sony or Roxio, to name a few. In these more complex programs you can insert old family films that have been digitized, video footage, audio clips, photos, images of documents, narration and music in the background. Before purchasing, you can compare programs and features online; type into your search engine: "video editing software."

The remainder of this chapter will focus on creating three distinct video projects all telling the same story: a simple, no frills digital photo album done in PowerPoint; a slightly more complex photo album with background music done in Windows Movie Maker; and a multifaceted documentary style piece that includes photos, audio clips, narration and music done in Pinnacle Studio 16.

You can view all three examples by going to my website: getcreativewithyourfamilyhistory.com. All tell the same story, but progress from simple to elaborate. I chose to tell the story of my Worthington ancestors with a big part of the story devoted to a brick home three generations of them lived in. By watching the three versions, you can see how different software, details and effort can increase the pleasure of viewing your family history.

Simple Digital Photo Album in PowerPoint

No doubt many of you have already used PowerPoint for various purposes. Family photo albums can be easily constructed in a simple straightforward style; unadorned if you like, or enhanced with creative special effects. Some of the options provided by PowerPoint include background colors, font styles and sizes, blank pages or templates, and transitions between images; you can add music or narration to a PowerPoint project.

In PowerPoint you can build slides (or pages) by inserting images, documents, and short pieces of identifying text. What you cannot do is insert large bodies of text. My solution was to type genealogy lists or other informational pages in a Word document.

Once the text has been thoroughly proofread and is to your satisfaction, make a digital copy. Save the original in your work file, then convert the copy to a PDF by scrolling down on the "save-as" and saving it as a PDF for insertion to the PowerPoint slide. Saving the original in your work file is like having insurance. If for some reason you need to reconstruct your PowerPoint file, you will still have a copy of the original to work with.

When your slide show is finished, read through and check again for spelling and date errors. Make any corrections. Save your work. Your project is now viewable on your computer. To share with family members or to view on a TV screen, your next step is to convert your PowerPoint slides to JPEGS (Joint Photographic Experts Groups) by using the "save as a JPEG" option. Drop the converted PowerPoint slides into a movie making software program, then follow the prompts to burn to a DVD.

If you are like me, and have little experience working with these programs, I encourage you to take some time to "play" before starting your project. I started on PowerPoint with a few photos, spending time exploring the options for layouts, backgrounds, font styles and sizes. I found PowerPoint easy to use and my confidence increased as I explored different functions while building my trial album.

Windows Movie Maker Provides More Options

Another commonly used piece of software is Windows Movie Maker. It too can be used to assemble an interesting family album with more embellishments than PowerPoint. In any movie maker software you can add video clips, music, narration, traditional photos and scanned documents. Windows Movie Maker is also easy to use, but functions very differently from PowerPoint. PowerPoint is made up of still slides for a presentation whereas Windows Movie Maker, or any other movie software, does exactly what it says: it makes a movie.

When you open Windows Movie Maker you will see a timeline track at the bottom of the screen. This is the movie track and includes separate lines for images, transitions, titles and a soundtrack. Import your scanned photos, documents, video and audio tapes into the Movie Maker project. They will be saved in the imported media section. As you create the movie you can then drag and drop the appropriate images into the movie timeline.

I highly encourage you to put together a sample movie before starting on your family project. During my own learning process I inserted photos and a commercially prepared video clip into the movie software. Movie Maker, like PowerPoint, does not allow for large bodies of text; so I constructed pages of text in a Word document, then converted them to JPEGS before inserting into the project. Movie programs generally require JPEGS instead of PDFs.

One thing I did struggle with for a while was how to insert captions in a systematic and easy to read manner. I found that by inserting the same photo twice, back to back, I could adjust the time sequence for one photo to appear for several seconds for easy viewing, then place an overlay of identifying comments on the second photo. The program allows you to choose as much time for viewing each photo as you desire.

To provide background music you will need to choose the music you want, import to your computer, then to the movie maker project. I found music on a Public Domain site that fit the tone I was trying to set for my story. Once the music is imported into the project you are working on, you can drag and drop onto the music sound track.

As with any print project, proofread thoroughly to make sure spellings and dates are correct. When you are satisfied that everything is accurate and complete, follow the prompts to "make the movie" then burn the DVD. You can make a creative disc cover or write on the disc itself. Be sure to include your name and date along with the title of your DVD.

Enhanced Documentary Style Project

My husband and I chose to create our most enhanced version of these three digital projects using Pinnacle Studio 16. The basic working premise of major movie making products is the same; we used Pinnacle software because my husband was already familiar with the program. Remember, use what you already know when possible.

After choosing your software, gather all your materials. Using the same process I used when making my Windows Movie Maker project, I first made images of genealogical information in a Word document, then converted them to JPEGs.

The next step is to prepare a detailed outline so you have a sequential order for dropping your photos and documents into the project. Choose a clear beginning point, a smooth flow of information in the middle and a definitive ending of the story.

Open your movie making program and import all of your material. Then, in order, drop the photo and text images into the movie track in the appropriate sections.

If you choose to narrate, you will need a script and a microphone. Some computers have built in microphones that will work. If yours does not, plug your external microphone into the microphone jack on your computer.

I put together a general outline of the images I wanted to present, the order in which I wanted the story to unfold and then wrote the script to match. We inserted an audio clip of my mother telling about the home where she grew up and displayed photos correlating to that house.

Once we had our images lined up, the script written and the audio tape ready to insert, we began practicing on the timing. To sync the script and the images, I read the script out loud while my husband adjusted the length of the images. You most likely can do this by yourself, but it is very helpful to have a partner.

Practice with a microphone before you begin recording. It took several tries for me to find the right position of the microphone. Speak slowly and distinctly. If your house is as busy as mine, you might consider a sign on the door saying "do not disturb!" Turn off the phones while you are recording.

The last thing you will do is to insert the track of background music. You can choose to use the music all the way through or just in certain sections. We used background music throughout the clip except during the audio portion of my mother's voice. It's a personal choice.

Once the project is complete, and to your satisfaction, follow the prompts to make the movie. Burn to a DVD. Identify your work by making a cover, or by printing your name, date and the title of the project on the disc.

If you have never worked with movie making software before, start small and work your way up. If you don't feel comfortable doing it by yourself, ask for help. Find a friend or a relative who would be willing to assist you. Most young adults have a solid grasp of computer technologies and can learn quickly if they are not already well versed in video making.

If you have already looked at the three examples for this chapter, you will realize they are not Hollywood production quality. My husband and I are not professionals. We do the work in our home office on our desktop PCs. We enjoy the challenges, and try our best to create interesting family videos that are enjoyable to watch.

Your production, like ours, doesn't have to be Oscar worthy to feel like it is valuable. If you have never done this kind of work, it may require repeated attempts to achieve the quality you are hoping for. Don't give up. Whether you choose to do digital albums or movies, I am absolutely certain that after your project is complete you will sit back and revel in your accomplishment. Your family members will appreciate your efforts also.

A while back, one of our family members made a family

documentary that just took my breath away. I was totally absorbed by the images, the narration and the stories. It was an incredible experience drawing me into the story through both images and sound, which a printed version of the same story lacks. As soon as I saw it, I knew I wanted to do something similar.

I hope you too will be inspired to bring your own stories to life through the use of video. We may be presenting the old world, but we are presenting it with new world technology. Our lives on the big screen!

Things I Have Learned Along the Journey

Life is an incredible journey. Life as the family archivist and story preserver brings that realization sharply into focus as I research, explore and chronicle various family histories. Those of us who choose this work are the keepers and promoters of our own journeys along with those of our ancestors.

Somehow, I knew when I was around 12 years old that one day I would write a book about my father's family. I remember sitting at the kitchen table, listening to the stories he and his brothers told. A few were sad, but most of the stories were told with hearty laughter, voices raised in loving camaraderie, happy recollections overflowing from their memory banks. I resolved then to record those funny and cherished memories; however, I almost waited too long.

When I finally got around to writing the *Korn Krops*, I was 50 years old. Many of the stories were lost. Many relatives were gone. It's one of my biggest regrets in life that I didn't start that project sooner. I can say the same thing about my mother's family story.

So here's the point. If you too are interested in putting your family story in writing, do not wait another day!

For nearly twenty years now, I have been pursuing the histories of my families and recording them through words, pictures and documentation. It's been an amazing adventure; and also a learning experience. If this is a new journey for you, you will no doubt have some questions and apprehensions as you embark on this odyssey. Here are some things I have learned along the way.

1. Do Not Wait Another Day!

I have already told you my own story about waiting too long. Friends often say to me, "Yes, I need to talk to my mother's sister (or brother, or whomever), but I just haven't had the time!" If you really want the stories, do not wait. Get on the phone, write letters or go visit your relatives. No one knows what tomorrow holds.

2. Accept the fact that you will make mistakes.

Every time I have completed a family project I read it over and over, have someone else read it, yet I still find mistakes after it is printed.

Proofreading is essential, read and re-read. Spell and grammar check are fantastic tools that help reduce mistakes. Use them. Even so, it's nearly impossible to produce a flawless piece. The most difficult items for me are dates. It is so easy to miss dates when proofreading. As soon as I type a date into a manuscript, I check it against the original in an attempt to minimize mistakes. But, it still happens. Accept it. Your family will forgive you.

3. Don't let writing skill concerns stop you.

Don't worry about your writing skills, your grammar or your spelling. Spell check and grammar check are a writer's best friends when composing on a computer. If you truly feel the need to educate yourself, you can find sources online with rules of grammar. You can also use a dictionary and thesaurus on the computer or keep hard copies handy. Please realize that the primary concern here is putting your family history in writing. Most family members will not be watching for style or spelling and grammatical errors. They will be grateful for the information.

4. Put your name and a date on all of your projects.

It is nice to be recognized for your work, but that is not the primary reason for identifying yourself in your work. Years from now when your descendants are pouring over something you put together they will want to know where it came from.

My mother's ancestors were very good about recording thoughts, stories and family information. Most of them did put their names and dates on what they wrote. But I remember finding a short piece written about the home they lived in with no identifying information other than "me." Fortunately there were only five siblings in the family, so I was able to track down the writer through a cousin. But it isn't always so simple. Please spare someone in future years from agonizing over who wrote what. Sign and date it now.

5. Save your work on the computer frequently.

For those of you who work on the computer regularly you already understand this. For those of you who may be new to putting together large bodies of work on a computer, it is essential that you save your work often. There is nothing more frustrating than to spend hours working on a piece and then lose it. Hit that save button often!

6. What do you do about family skeletons?

This is a tough question that, truly, only you can answer. I can tell you how I have handled things.

First and foremost, I believe the writer must be true to the family history. However, I also believe the writer has the responsibility to see the bigger picture of any individual within the family and assess whether telling the whole truth is essential. If your ancestor was convicted of a crime, or involved in questionable activities, you probably will need to deal with that somehow in your story. But do you really need to tell the whole unvarnished truth about family members who have merely been less than stellar?

Several years ago I wrote a short story about a favorite uncle. He was a kind, loving, charming man, and fun to be around. But, like all human beings, he had his faults. He was financially irresponsible; and undercurrents of family gossip kept alive the notion that he had at one time embezzled some money. By the time I was an adult the story could no longer be corroborated or refuted, but I used it in the story in an effort to be true to his character.

A few years later I was with three of his granddaughters who had never known him at all. They were hungry to know about their deceased grandfather. I remembered the story I had written and sent each of them a copy without thinking about the embezzling allegation. The granddaughters loved the story. They assured me afterward that the insinuations did not destroy the joy of learning about their grandfather, but rather underscored the knowledge that all of us have flaws.

I felt guilty. In an effort to be true to his character, I had imparted information that tarnished his image in the eyes of granddaughters he had never known. Even though the unconfirmed story had long been part of the family lore, I wished fervently that I had left it out.

Since then I have deliberately left out other pieces of family stories that I believe were inconsequential to the overall history of the family. A particularly gruesome accident involving the three-year-old child of my great-great-grandparents didn't add anything to the essence of their story. So I left it out.

If one of your ancestors was truly incorrigible, you will no doubt want to deal with that openly and honestly within the manuscript. Character flaws, however, are inherent in each of us making our families interesting and colorful. You are the only one who can decide what to include and what to omit out of consideration for your loved ones.

Being the family archivist has been a wonderful learning experience for me. I have eagerly delved into the ancestral lines, discovered bits and pieces of their stories and became enthralled as I envisioned their lives within the historical context of those eras.

I have also learned that my family appreciates my efforts. By nature, no one else in my family is interested in doing this kind of work that I love so much. But they absolutely are interested in the results of my work. They love the pictures. They love the stories.

My cousin Becky kept her copy of the *Korn Krops* on her living room table and looked at it regularly. She updated information, inserted obituaries and paper clipped news articles within the pages of the *Korn Krops*. It was a well-used book until her death.

My cousin Judy sent me a thank you note after receiving her copy of the Worthington pictorial history. She said, "There is so much we would not know if you hadn't done these books."

I would do the work anyway. But knowing that my family enjoys and appreciates my work is gratifying.

Family history is never ending, and I am already watching my grandchildren to see which of them will discover the joy of capturing their family history. Then again, it may be one of their children who discovers the joy and satisfaction of preserving and passing along our family stories. The pen will be passed eventually as the story continues to unfold.

Your story continues too. If you don't record it, who will? Don't let your family history slip into oblivion. Collect those stories today, and get creative with your family history!

Notes

Glossary

DPI

DPI stands for dots per inch which directly influence the clarity and resolution of your photos. The higher the density of the DPI, the better your photo will appear when you print it. Scanners should be set to the highest setting for the best quality. Keep in mind that it will also increase the amount of ink used to print the photo if you are doing your own printing.

Format

The use of the word format throughout this book should not be confused with the computer term which means preparing a disc for use. Instead, I use the term in reference to the general appearance of any given project or publication: that is, a form, design, or arrangement of your information, photos, and documents. You can present your information in a book, photo album, calendar, greeting card, or a DVD. Each of these is a type of format that will display your family history in the form you desire.

Landscape Orientation

Landscape orientation refers to the position of the paper you are working on. When you hold a piece of 8½ by 11 inch paper in your hands, landscape position occurs when the 11 inch width is at the top and bottom of the page, 8½ inches to the sides; in other words, landscape orientation is wider than it is tall. When working on a computer, you can choose landscape orientation in the page settings section when formatting your page.

JPEG (Joint Photographic Experts Group)

There are many image file formats, but JPEGS are the most common. These images are compressed in a 10 to 1 ratio providing quality color and clarity when printed. JPEGS are images on a camera, a scan, or web-based documents that are downloaded onto your computer and then inserted into any manuscript.

PDF

PDF stands for Portable Document Format created by Adobe Systems. I use it primarily when I need to move a file from one piece of software to another, such as making slides on Word, then moving it to a

PowerPoint document; or from Publisher to a Word manuscript. A PDF can be opened in multiple software programs. To convert your document to a PDF, merely do a "save as," click on PDF, and the computer will automatically convert your Word, Publisher or other type of manuscript. Once your document has been converted to a PDF file, you cannot make changes unless you have specific Adobe software.

Portrait Orientation

Portrait orientation refers to the position of the paper you are working on. When you hold a piece of 8½ by 11 inch paper in your hands, portrait position occurs when the 8½ inch width is at the top and bottom of the page, 11 inch length to the sides; in other words, portrait orientation is taller than it is wide. When working on a computer, you can choose portrait orientation in the page settings section when formatting your page.

Public Domain

The term Public Domain refers to any creative works that are free from copyright or patent restrictions and therefore usable by the public. Patented and copyrighted materials cannot be used without permission. The background music used in my example DVD is from the Public Domain site: Incompetech.com.

Scoring

Scoring is a technique used with heavier paper such as cardstock to make a fold neater and crisper. Lay your cardstock flat. I like to lay it on a paper cutter so I can line it up with the measurements on the bed of the cutter. Find the place you want to fold your paper and lay a ruler along that line. Using an X-acto knife, or similar tool, use the backside of the blade and slightly press onto the paper along the line. You will not be cutting the paper, but merely scratching the surface so that you can easily fold and crease along the line you have made.

Search Engine

A search engine is a computer program that enables someone to find information on the World Wide Web (WEB) by using a word search. Primary examples of search engines are Google and Yahoo.

Template

A template is a pattern. I use this term throughout the book in reference to the layout of a page that I am designing on the computer. Some software programs offer commercially prepared templates you can find within that particular program, such as Word or Publisher. I also use the term in reference to making my own page designs. I have greeting card templates, stationary templates, and calendar templates saved in folders on my computer. When I am ready to create a new greeting card, I can do a "save as' into a new document which allows me to create a different card using the original template.

Notes

Acknowledgments

There are many people to acknowledge and thank for helping me put this book together. Writing a book may seem like a solitary endeavor, and much of it is, but writing a book does require a certain amount of interaction between the writer and the larger world: for doing research, listening to the people who critique the work, and paying attention to both the positive and negative comments of all who have encouraged me.

First of all, I am deeply indebted to my ancestors. My mother's family came to America in the 1600s. From the very beginning they were obviously aware that recording their ancestral lines, legacies and stories would have lasting value. I am grateful to all of them for their foresight.

My mother, like me, was fascinated by genealogy and the family stories that went along with it. She collected boxes of information that made my own research and writing much easier. Thank you, Mom!

I am grateful to my many friends who have taken an interest in this book. My faithful readers and dispassionate critics are Dadee Burdick, Judi Finkenbine Fisher, Howard Jenkins, Lorraine McCracken, Arthur Ross and Mark Maxwell. All of you supplied the extra "eyes and brains" that I needed to keep me striving for a more concise and readable book.

I also want to thank Janis Foley, friend and fellow pursuer of genealogy and family history; also Professor Roy Finkenbine, head of the History Department at University of Detroit Mercy Campus in Michigan. They were both extremely helpful with genealogical resources.

Special thanks to my children and grandchildren for their support and encouragement. My two high-tech sons, Jeff Niggemeyer and John Niggemeyer, have willingly shared insights and comments regarding computer terms and technical aspects of the projects within this book. My daughter, Jennifer Stephens, plus family members Kirk, Michelle, and Anne have all encouraged me in my writing endeavors.

I am especially grateful to Anne Gundersen, my daughter-in-law, for designing the cover of this book. Her years of experience in graphic design have certainly benefited me.

Betty Westby has been my "right hand girl." Even before I began writing this book, Betty and I shared an interest in genealogy and family history. We worked on family history projects at the same time, sharing ideas and encouraging one another. She has supported me in this endeavor in so many ways: by reading and critiquing my manuscript, by sharing some of her own work within this book, and most of all for her continuous confidence that my talent would be equal to the task of putting this book together.

My "right hand man" has been my husband, Chuck. I couldn't ask for a more ardent supporter. For many years Chuck has witnessed my passion for family history, has enjoyed the family books I have put together and encouraged me to put my experiences in writing for others to draw from. Beyond his encouragement, Chuck has been instrumental in helping put together the digital versions that can be found on my website. For many years now his creative talent for making interesting videos has added immeasurably to the family archives.

www.ingramcontent.com/pod-product-compliance
Lightning Source LLC
Chambersburg PA
CBHW020441290526
45785CB00002B/951